Faith Shaping Ministry

Faith Shaping Ministry

PAUL E. HOFFMAN

Foreword by the Reverend Dr. Christian Scharen

CASCADE *Books* · Eugene, Oregon

FAITH SHAPING MINISTRY

Cascade Books
An Imprint of Wipf and Stock Publishers
199 W. 8th Ave., Suite 3
Eugene, OR 97401

www.wipfandstock.com

ISBN 13: 978-1-62032-582-7

Cataloguing-in-Publication Data

Hoffman, Paul E.

Faith shaping ministry / Paul E. Hoffman ; foreword by Christian Scharen.

xvi + 118 p. ; 23 cm. Includes bibliographical references.

ISBN 13: 978-1-62032-582-7

1. Initiation rites—Religious aspects—Christianity. 2. Baptism—Lutheran
Church. 3. Catechumens—Lutheran Church. I. Scharen, Christian Batalden.

BV813.3 .H64 2013

Manufactured in the U.S.A.

For Pastor Stan and Jan Ecklund
with my deepest thanks
for the many ways that you formed my faith
and shaped my ministry

Contents

Foreword

I HAVE PONDERED what attracts so many young adults in the United States to the Icelandic band Sigur Rós. Their songs regularly stretch over the ten-minute mark, clearly far beyond the supposed attention span of the new media generation. Sometimes described simultaneously as "post-rock" and "post-classical," they frustrate attempts at labels in an era of microcategories fitted to every taste. And to top it off, they mostly sing in Icelandic, a language spoken by few people anywhere outside of their small North Atlantic island home. Not that it helps much when they don't sing in Icelandic. For those songs, they sing in a made-up vocalization they've named "Vonlenska," which translates to "Hopelandic." Yet against all conventional assumptions about what will connect, Sigur Rós connects profoundly. Their music, one young blogger said, is like "bringing heaven to earth."

Similar ponderings arise when I consider why so many people with fragile and broken connections to religion find themselves (sometimes surprisingly) drawn into Phinney Ridge Lutheran Church in Seattle. Not a church to keep the service neatly under one hour, and steadfastly opposed to having Sunday school concurrent with worship, they clearly missed the memo about people not putting up with this any longer. A self-described traditional church but with emergent sensibilities, hosting great choral works and unabashed liturgical worship but with a barista whipping up lattes to take into the pews, Phinney Ridge confounds efforts to pigeonhole within a market niche. They steadfastly speak in the language of word and sacrament, of lectionary and life, of Christ's invitation to die and be born anew. They do not make accessible translations to meet people at their level of understanding but rather make of themselves accessible translations of the Gospel to each stranger who comes. Yet against all conventional wisdom about what makes churches hip and attractive, Phinney Ridge connects profoundly. In their life together, as one teen said, "You can dress and act like who you really are—a child of God."

A common thread: both Sigur Rós and Phinney Ridge offer us "more." In a culture saturated with spin and glitter, jaded eyes see shallow a mile away. Many people are on the lookout for places with a depth able to cope with the real longings and hopes within us. So "more"—and also "depth." I can imagine lead singer Jón Þór Birgisson, aka Jónsi, or lead pastor Paul Hoffman, asking someone new to their respective arts: "Welcome. How deep would you like to go?" In the case of Phinney Ridge, the awful and freeing truth is this: deep enough to die. Drowning is not the most obvious marketing ploy for a church looking not only to survive but to thrive, but there you have it. Churches are tempted to simply say, "Come all you who are thirsty. Come to the waters of life." Such invitations are not fully honest. Phinney Ridge could legitimately begin a billboard campaign saying: "Come, all you who seek God, and die." Yet for the fullness of their God-given good news to be translated, the rest of the invitation must be said. "Come, all you who seek God, and die, so you may be born anew to the life that really is life."

Reading this lovely book is like catching a vision of the life that really is life. And it is a primer in ways to participate with God in living the life we come to know in Christ Jesus, offered through the Spirit in baptism. The ripples of baptismal water, Paul argues, wash over every aspect of congregational life. In response to congregational decline and increasing secularity in the culture, Phinney Ridge decided against novel programs and instead, in a thorough and intentional way, followed the pattern of the faithful stretching all the way back to the fourth century of Christianity. Called the "catechumenate" or, at Phinney Ridge, "The WAY," this intentional welcoming of newcomers to baptism and life in Christian community has formed faith for newcomer and old-timer alike. Some might well argue that those ancient Christians who began the catechumenate did so because they faced missional challenges in a pluralistic and sometimes hostile culture—dynamics quite similar to the contemporary "post-Christian" context in the United States!

But a warning before you dive in: don't read this wonderful, moving, simple yet deep book by yourself. No one person can turn a ship around; it takes the whole crew. Gather a group from your congregation and commit to reading and conversation together. *Faith Shaping Ministry* is an awesome—and practical—depiction of shared lay and clergy leadership that declares, "Renewal of life and ministry in your congregation is not only possible, but God's dream for you."

For you, but not only for *you*. For those you do not yet know, as well. For those who have not yet visited your church, but for whom you pray. Near the heart of the book, Paul describes the worry many have in turning the church upside down for people who aren't even present (yet) and who might (when they come) change things! In answer to these worries, we hear perhaps the most beautiful and powerful argument for engaging in the baptismal renewal *Faith Shaping Ministry* calls for:

> People come week in and week out seeking something of which they are not quite certain. But they will recognize the presence of Christ—the genuine, healing, welcoming presence of Christ—as we offer it as best as our gifts allow in an intentional and thoughtful way. God's people deserve such a welcome. God's people are called to offer such a welcome, one to another.

The good news is that such a vision is simple, and at hand. It is not easy, of course! But what we need, Paul tells us, God has given us already: "Word and water, wine and wheat, font, table, pulpit, prayers and sermon, song and silence." God's baptismal mystery is there, transforming us from death to life, reconciling a broken world crying out for healing. What we need, I think, are fearless leaders who, like Sigur Rós and Phinney Ridge, risk the question, "How deep would you like to go?"

The Reverend Dr. Christian Scharen

Acknowledgments

WITH A PROFOUND sense of gratitude to God, I begin these brief notes of thanks with my parents who, against all odds, were diligent in their baptismal promises on my behalf and provided a model of faithful living at home and a committed example of service in church and community. Although my dad died in 1971, his words and actions of faith live on in my memory, and Mom's example at age ninety-three is still powerful and exceptional. I am so grateful.

From their home to my own, the transition was smooth. I have been blessed by my wife and partner, Donna, whose parallel faith development and life of service has been an inspiration and a joy. Her insights in ministry, many of which are reflected in these pages, have certainly shaped and formed my own.

The congregation of Phinney Ridge Lutheran Church in Seattle is an amazing place to do ministry. With an unceasing sense of commitment and adventure, God's people in this community of faith have been bold to proclaim the Gospel of Jesus in a new age. At the same time, we have found that the best tools for that shared mission have been the treasures of the church across the centuries: Scripture, word and sacrament, and a historic, yet nuanced, sense of our tradition. It is counterintuitive to think of one's congregation as emergent and traditional, yet this is exactly how we describe ourselves.

In the preparation of this manuscript, I am grateful to the shared work of these pastoral colleagues: the Reverend Sallie Shippen, the Reverend Nathan Baker-Trinity, and the Reverend John Carlson. I share my gratitude as well with Lois Huseby, one of the most faithful women and careful proofreaders I have ever

Acknowledgments

met. The guidance and nurture of Charlie Collier and Jacob Martin at Wipf and Stock is a precious gift.

Finally, I want to reach out to my partners in ministry over the years, all those with whom I have served and whose collaborative work has formed faith and shaped ministry. To the associates, the interns, the musical, ministry, and office staff persons: I trust you know that our shared work is written between every line. I am particularly grateful to my colleague and associate in ministry for my work at Phinney Ridge, the Reverend Beverly Piro. I am confident that the partnership that we cherish will continue to flourish as we serve the church in new and different ways. Thanks be to God.

Preface
Yes, Really. *Living* Water

THIS IS THE story of how one congregation's ministry was completely transformed by intentionally choosing to focus on offering new Christians the gift of holy baptism. For the past twenty years, Phinney Ridge Lutheran Church in Seattle has been practicing a version of the ancient church's pattern of forming new Christians. This pattern has been adapted and nuanced to fit the call to mission that we perceive in our own time, living as we do in one of the most secular cities in North America. Grounded in the conviction that faith comes from hearing, our ancestors in the faith called the process the Catechumenate, a word that has its roots in the Greek *catecheo,* meaning "to resound in the ear."

What we've discovered about bringing new Christians to the font is that baptismal water ebbs and flows. So while we at first imagined that we would offer the opportunity to become disciples to people new to Christian faith, what we ended up learning was that by doing this, the *ebb* of God's grace came back to us. We who were offering a gift in the name of Jesus were transformed as well. Not only that, now that we've been practicing this intentional style of ministry for twenty years, we have a congregation that is immersed in the theology and the wonder of baptismal living. The pattern that Martin Luther urged us to make a pattern of *daily* life—the pattern of dying to sin and rising to new life that is at the heart of Romans 6—has become evident throughout the various ministries, practices, and programs of congregational life among us.

Building upon the work of the first volume in this series, called simply *Faith Forming Faith,* this book's goal is to show how offering

Preface

baptism and affirmation of baptism to newcomers in our parish as an intentional practice has transformed most, if not all, aspects of our ministry. Like water running over rock, the grounding of our faith and life in the waters of baptism has slowly but irrevocably shaped who we are and how our parish life is organized. And, like water running over rock, the shifts in our community of faith were gradual, every now and then punctuated by a more substantial shift like the kind that comes when rocks are washed about the creek bed after heavy rain.

The thanks for these shifts in practice that have led to joy and vitality belongs to God alone. As we have made an effort to more intentionally focus on the renewing and transformative gifts that stir in the waters of the font, we have rediscovered the gifts that the first Christians handed on to us with such conviction: worship, Scripture study, prayer, and the work of ministry in the world. The act of being dead to self and alive to God in Christ Jesus is the aim. Sin, in its many manifestations among us, holds us back, of course, as it would any community of faith. But here's the goal: that every activity of parish life flow out of and back to the font. That any music, any ritual, any action, any decoration or innovation, any sermon, any prayer, any program, ministry, or work that we might do in the name of Jesus be imagined and purposed to follow his very own pattern of death and resurrection. *For if we have been united with him in a death like his, we shall surely be united with him in a resurrection like his.* (Romans 6:5)

So the following pages suggest a pattern of parish life that ebbs and flows to and from the font, just as our congregation itself does week in and week out. You can imagine that as we gather to confess our failings and be renewed with the gift of life, that same pattern of baptismal living—ebbing in for renewal, then flowing out to serve—is at the heart of how we are coming to understand our parish's mission and work. Whether that work be Bible study or parish administration, outreach to the neighbor in need or education of one another in the riches of Christ—whether it be oriented toward worship, learning, or service—it is our hope that the ministry starts and ends in the water, for the water is storied with the Word. And the Word is Christ.

Paul E. Hoffman
Seattle, Washington
November 1, 2012

I

And a Little Child Shall Lead Them

JUST A FEW weeks ago, Brigid's mom and stepdad came to me after the second service and asked if we could say a prayer together. Brigid was flying from Seattle all the way to Chicago to spend two months of summer vacation with her father. It was the first time that she and her mom had been apart for so long, and even though her stepdad asked me to say a prayer for Brigid, I was pretty sure that the prayer was for them as well.

Brigid was being her usual kindergarten self, bouncing around the narthex of the church from adult to adult and from kid to kid. This was her new family of faith, those to whom she had endeared herself in the past nine months since moving with her mom and stepdad to Seattle.

Following the parents' request, I got on my knees, called her over, and told her: "Mom and Michael think it would be a good idea for us to say a prayer together before you fly to Chicago tomorrow for the summer. What do you think about that?"

And then the most amazing thing happened: Brigid took me by the hand, motioned to her mom and stepdad to follow, and led the three of us into the sanctuary to the baptismal font.

She dipped her hand into the water, made the sign of the cross and then looked up at the three of us as if to say, "Okay. Let's get this prayer underway."

Brigid knew to go to the font because of what she had heard. In Romans 10, St. Paul reminds us that *faith comes from what is heard, and what is heard comes through the word of Christ.* What Brigid heard had come to her in a lifetime of caring faith formation from her parents, fulfilling the promises made for her in holy baptism. What Brigid heard came to her in the Bible stories that were read and told to her. What Brigid heard had been reinforced through the last several months' worth of faith formation that she had received in children's choir.

> I've just come from the fountain,
> I've just come from the fountain, Lord,
> I've just come from the fountain,
> his name's so sweet.[1]

What she had heard had been dramatically revealed to her a few months earlier in the powerful liturgy of the Easter Vigil. The transformative, saving action of moving from death to new life in Christ that stands at the heart of the Christian gospel had been spoken and demonstrated to her in a weekly confessional rite. There she saw water poured into the font, then ritually sprinkled as the words of forgiveness were announced in the name of Jesus.

While all of us in parish ministry may not yet fully know or appreciate it, we have congregations full of Brigids: women, children, and men who have heard the faith proclaimed and who have the potential to live in such a way that all roads lead to the living, transforming Christ in the baptismal waters. We have congregations filled with Brigids: men and women, children and youth who are eager to live out a faith that is born in baptism's waters. From those waters we draw the life of Christ, crucified and risen from the dead, to propel us into the world to serve. What our Brigids need is a style of leadership that takes this promise and conviction seriously and puts it into practice in ways that permeate all of parish life.

That pattern of dying and rising is the pattern of life given to us by Christ himself. It is a pattern given us by the very first Christians as witnessed by Paul's strong and beautiful embrace of

1. "I've Just Come from the Fountain," arr. by James Capers, in *With One Voice,* #696.

that pattern throughout Romans 6. It is a pattern that lived on in the church's early history as witnessed by Cyril, bishop of Jerusalem, in the fourth century: *The waters of baptism were at once your grave and your Mother.*[2] These interwoven images of death and new life are inextricably united. Here is the clear pattern for Christian life that is truly transformative: dying to the old life of sin and rising out of the waters into a new life as disciples of Jesus formed for service in the world.

It is all grounded in the font, and it is all in the font because the Word is grounded in the font. And the Word is grounded in the font because Christ is in the font.

> Do you not know that all of us who have been baptized into Christ Jesus were baptized into his death? Therefore we have been buried with him by baptism into death, so that, just as Christ was raised from the dead by the glory of the Father, so we too might walk in newness of life. For if we have been united with him in a death like his, we shall certainly be united with him in a resurrection like his. (Rom 6:3–5)

In this bold new vision of living in the ancient Christians' pattern of faith formation, we must see our life in church as fully immersed in the wonder of baptism. I propose that we rethink parish life in such a way that all we do is shaped by a reappropriation of our most basic and formative paradigm—the death and resurrection of Jesus, to which each of us is joined in our baptism. This is not to make baptism a new god. Neither is it to abandon any of the classic categories of theological conversation that we all love and cherish—law and gospel, sin and grace, repentance and forgiveness. It is instead to richly embrace them and to be absolutely certain, to the best of our abilities, that these classic categories are doing nothing less than serving the saving gospel, for the sake of the transformation of the world.

In her latest work, *Christianity after Religion*, Diana Butler Bass wisely and convincingly makes the case that we have entered

---

2. *Cat.* 20.4. Cited by Kreider, *Change of Conversion and the Origin of Christendom*, 45.

a post-Christian era in North American life. When someone or something has died, a rebirth is in order.[3] So perhaps the key to our new life in the present and exciting era of Christian faith is to become like a little child. To become like Brigid: taking one another's hands, skipping to the source of life, undeterred and unafraid of the death that lurks at the edges of the font—our grave and our mother—because, after all, what is left to fear in death? Perhaps we could be like Brigids in our shared and important walk into a new way of doing ministry. Taking one another's hands, could we be unabashedly unafraid, for the sake of the gospel, to dip into the saving waters and let those waters drip, trickle, run, and perhaps even gush over us and into a needy world?

On the pages that follow, the story of one congregation's ministry in a very secular city is chronicled. Our story is offered so that you, too, might find renewal and new life in the very core activities of parish life: confirmation, pre-marital preparation, worship planning, preaching, administration, Sunday school, and so many more. In each of these areas of ministry it is hoped that you can imagine your parish skipping to the waters of the font, finding there a renewal of faith and life, and then joyously going into the world to serve with renewed energy, conviction, and hope.

3. Bass, *Christianity after Religion*, 28.

2

A Word about The WAY

Before unfolding the story of how offering new Christians the gift of holy baptism has changed our congregational life, it will be important to give a brief overview of the process itself. We call this year of intentional faith formation The WAY.

For two decades, visitors, friends, potential members, unbaptized Christians, and people seeking a deeper spiritual life have gathered together on Sunday evenings for a meal and Bible study. From October through Pentecost, all people who are "inquiring" about faith and life in our parish are directed toward this process. For some it is their very first encounter with Christians and Christianity. For others, perhaps active Lutherans all their lives, it is an opportunity for a "faith sabbatical." Most people fall somewhere in the middle of these two descriptions—people for whom baptism took place long ago and far away. For reasons as varied as the people themselves, their baptismal life never went much beyond the day that the sacrament was administered.

Our parish's commitment to the first group, the unbaptized, grew out of the realization that our parish was no longer growing or even self-sustaining. The thousands of members in 1960 who were worshiping weekly had diminished to less than three hundred in the early 1990s. We were no longer repopulating the parish in the usual Lutheran ways—through birth and through immigration from northern European nations. Combine that with ministering in the city of Seattle, where the vast majority of the population when asked will list "None" as their religious preference,[1] and you have a rich mission field for forming faith and bringing people to the waters of baptism. In what has turned out to be a tremendous gift of the Holy Spirit's leadership among us, we chose to do this in a thorough and intentional way following the pattern of the faithful that stretches all the way back to the fourth century. Grace, wisdom, and care prevailed in our decision-making, and the congregation and its leaders resisted the option of "baptism on demand." Clearly, offering the sacrament with little or no prior formation in the current religious environment was neither pastoral nor effective in shaping the lives of new Christians.

As our new process of faith formation began in the early nineties, there simply weren't people lining up at our door to be baptized. So in an effort to have a viable, sustainable group with which to work, even those who would ordinarily have simply "transferred in" were given the opportunity to participate in the yearlong process of The WAY, and strongly encouraged to do so. In the early days of our practice, the men and women who would ordinarily have spent an hour or two in Pastor's Class were gifted with an entire year of Bible study, fellowship, and ritual welcome instead. Where they may have received a tour of the church and a box of offering envelopes, they received a renewing and life-giving year of welcome grounded in the Scriptures.

The great majority of people to whom we minister in The WAY are people who had been baptized as children, or perhaps as a result of a spiritual awakening in college or early adulthood, but had wandered away and lost interest in discipleship in Christ for one reason or another. Some were coming to us requesting baptism for their own children. Some came at a time of personal crisis—a death in the family, the loss of a job, a life-threatening illness. Some came looking for a place to have a wedding and received instead a year of formation in faith and a congregation in which to ground their marriage.

---

1. Killen and Silk, *Religion and Public Life in the Pacific Northwest*.

But the heart of the matter is that those who gathered and were invited to this substantial process of faith formation reflected the complexion of our neighborhood itself. They were men and women of a variety of backgrounds, with a variety of faith experiences, triumphs, challenges, and disappointments. They were bold or timid, well grounded in faith or hanging on by a thread, married or single, gay or straight, certain or deeply, *deeply* questioning.

The process and narrative of The WAY is thoroughly recounted in the first volume of this series, *Faith Forming Faith*. A quick review of it will assist you in making fuller use of the details provided in the present volume on how this process of bringing people to baptism, its affirmation, and beyond has shaped all of parish life.

Shortly after Easter, staff members begin to identify people like those described above and organize them into informal groups for the coming fall's process. A couple of social events, perhaps combined with a Bible study in the style of The WAY, are sometimes hosted in the summer months, but it is in October that the process begins in earnest.

On Sunday evenings in the fall, newcomers gather with current parish members for a fellowship meal and a small group Bible study from 5:00 to 7:00 P.M. Eventually each of the newcomers—called candidates early on in the process—is matched with a parish member who will walk with them throughout the course of this year as a sponsor. This sponsor will be by their side throughout the season of small group Bible studies, at the fellowship meals, for rituals that punctuate the process from time to time at Sunday liturgy, and—of course—at the time of their baptism or affirmation of baptism. In our case, baptism and affirmation take place at the Easter Vigil, a glorious and beautiful liturgy that is held the night before Easter, the ancient church's traditional time to welcome new Christians through the sacrament of baptism.

The meals served on Sunday evenings are well planned and robust; they are unhurried opportunities for conversation and welcome. These meals are themselves a significant part of the process of sharing the Christ-like gifts of welcome and hospitality.

Dinner is followed by more food—this time the participants feast on the Word. Gathering in groups of six to ten persons, and led by a lay Bible study leader, the small groups use the morning's preaching text from the Bible as their primary source of reflection. This is not the sort of Bible study in which everyone is to agree upon "what this text means." Instead, along with the morning's sermon, it is used as a springboard from which people are encouraged to bring their questions about faith: "Who *is* Jesus?" "Why do people suffer if God is love?" "Do I have to believe that Christ is the Son of God to belong here?" "What do you mean, 'resurrection of the body'?"

The pastors are not participants in the small group Bible studies. The groups are completely participant-directed and lay-led. The inquirers are accompanied by their sponsors, and the entire group is led by a catechist—a lay Bible study leader. Because of the style of the studies, the best-qualified lay leaders are not those who are biblical experts, but those who can read social dynamics well and have a non-anxious presence. If you've done the math, you've already deduced that there are more seasoned Christians than newcomers in each small group. With all these active parish members involved in the faith formation process, you can also probably already see why forming faith has had a huge role in shaping ministry.

Throughout the course of the newcomers' year of formation, they are often invited to come before the congregation, along with their sponsors, for welcome and prayer. Gathering around the font during the Sunday morning service, they learn by seeing for themselves that Christianity is not a private faith but a corporate one. The community is interested in their presence among us and routinely recognizes and prays for them as a sign of their inclusion into the body of Christ.

The Lenten season becomes a time of more intense preparation and decision-making for each inquirer. If they are candidates for baptism, this is the time in which they decide, in consultation with their sponsor and their pastors, that *this* Easter will be the time at which their baptism takes place. If they are preparing to affirm their baptism—having already been baptized in a previous congregation—they make the decision whether or not they are ready to stand before the congregation at the Easter Vigil, renounce the forces of evil, and affirm the power of the Risen Christ to create and sustain a life of faith and discipleship.

Lent is also the season in which most persons who are uncertain about their future as disciples of Jesus choose not to be baptized or to affirm their baptisms at the coming Easter celebration. Because this is a period of intense preparation, the questions are deeper, the demands of Christian life more clear, and the responsibilities about to be affirmed in public worship are more thoroughly examined, studied, and discussed. For some, a decision not to be baptized or to affirm means a departure from the congregation, having discovered that the Christian faith is not for them. For others, it means a continuation in worship and service without a present public commitment to embrace the baptized life. For the great majority of those who are not ready to continue, it means an even deeper immersion in their questions and the congregation's response. Their tendency is to enroll in a second (and sometimes even a third!) year of The WAY in order to explore life in Christ in greater depth.

The high point of the process is the celebration of Easter. The WAY is designed to correspond with St. Paul's baptismal theology spun out most richly in Romans 6. In particular, the process affirms that, being united to Christ through baptism in a death like his, we are united with him in a resurrection like his.

Following Easter, the small groups continue to meet on Sunday evenings in the same format with a slightly different slant: now that you've been baptized, or have affirmed your baptism, *what does this mean?* It's a time to explore more richly and fully how one lives out one's Christian convictions in daily life. *How does following Jesus shape my life as a worker, a spouse, a parent, a citizen of the world?*

Through the new and renewed Christians with whom God has entrusted us, baptismal, resurrection life has become the formational paradigm shaping our ministry. Having practiced Christian life as a catechumenal congregation for the past twenty years, our church now has in it a generation of people who are people of The WAY. Their influence, their gifts, their understanding of life in Christ have all profoundly influenced the shape of our lives together in Christ and the mission that we share in Jesus' name.

3

The Faith Formation of Jane

WITH SOME PRELIMINARY history and context about our congregation's challenge and response laid out, we can now move into a chronological view of how embracing a model of faith formation has shaped every aspect of our life in ministry.

As stated in the previous chapter (and repeated often in the pages that follow), our life is grounded in the death and resurrection of Jesus, laid out most clearly by Paul in Romans 6 and deeply woven into the fabric of our baptismal liturgy. This pattern of dying and rising forms the paradigm for a life that we are called to model as God's people. Both the promises from God and the commitments with which we respond are significant and are not embraced in the single moment of the sacrament's celebration, but are lived out across a lifetime of walking with the risen Christ. *Evangelical Lutheran Worship*'s baptismal liturgy makes the promises and responsibilities of the sacrament abundantly clear for parents, for sponsors, and for the congregation.

> In baptism our gracious heavenly Father frees us from sin and death by joining us to the death and resurrection of our Lord Jesus Christ. We are born children of a fallen humanity; by water and the Holy Spirit we are reborn children of God and made members of the church, the body of Christ. Living with Christ and in the communion

of saints, we grow in faith, love, and obedience to the will
of God.

As you bring [this child] to receive the gift of baptism, you are
entrusted with responsibilities:
>to live with them among God's faithful people,
>bring them to the word of God and the holy supper,
>teach them the Lord's Prayer, the Creed, and the Ten
>Commandments,
>place in their hands the holy scriptures,
>and nurture them in faith and prayer,
>so that [your children/this candidate] may learn to trust God,
>proclaim Christ through word and deed,
>care for others and the world God made,
>and work for justice and peace.[1]

Here is the story of how one child has been guided by parents
and congregation through the mysterious and wonderful journey
of baptism that began with their promises above, and by her washing in the font of Jesus' grace.

When Jane's parents discovered that they were expecting a
child, they began to inquire about the sacrament of baptism for
their awaited baby. They had been raised in the church and had
participated in the congregation's ministry of faith formation when
they prepared to affirm their baptisms several years before. Our
wisdom and experience has led us as pastors to avoid setting a date
or arranging other aspects of an infant baptismal celebration prior
to the birth of a child in our parish, so while Todd and Amy's request was received with joy, we counseled them to wait until the
baby arrived rather than allow these events to become concrete in
their own hearts and minds. Birth is a complicated process, and
when a difficult birth experience is compounded by a disappointing rearrangement of baptismal plans, the pain for parents can be
unnecessarily multiplied.

Once we all met and knew Jane, her baptism was scheduled
and carried out with joy and flourish. Baptisms occur at times other
than the Easter Vigil in our parish when the parents involved have

1. *Evangelical Lutheran Worship,* 228

11

already participated in The WAY or are longtime members of the body of Christ.

In grateful obedience to their baptismal promises, Jane's parents began to bring her to "the services of God's house" with regularity. This was not a stretch for them since their own worship practice as young adults was regular and robust. From the time that she was a babe in arms, Jane received a blessing at the communion table when her mom and dad received the Eucharist. As is parish practice, Todd or Amy also brought her forward each Sunday for Children's Word. We encourage this practice from birth so that there is never a time when children *can't* remember coming to receive the Word of God tailored specifically for them in Children's Word. It has been our experience that when a random age is set for children to begin participation in Children's Word or eucharistic ministries, then the beginning point can be intimidating or overwhelming for them. We encourage parents to model the expectation for their child that this is simply how life with Christ *is*, just as they would model wearing a seatbelt in a car or a helmet on a bike. We worship on Sundays. We experience others around us singing, praying, listening, confessing, and receiving forgiveness. We go to Children's Word. We receive a blessing or a meal at the Lord's table.

When Jane reached the age of three, she transitioned from nursery care during the education hour at our church and became a regular member of a Sunday school class. Along with her peers she began and continues to receive one phase of the "instruction in the Christian faith" that mom, dad, sponsors, and parish committed to when she was received into the community of faith as a baptized child of God. The language we use around Sunday school and confirmation ministries for Jane and her peers is the language of partnership. These responsibilities for education are neither the parents' nor the sponsors' alone to carry out. We *all* made a commitment to nurture each child in the Christian faith when the waters of baptism washed over him or her. Sunday school, Children's Word, vacation Bible school, and Wednesday evening midweek Bread for the Journey education classes are a variety of ways in which the congregation holds up its end of the covenant.

So far, none of the offerings in which Jane participated should seem all that odd to congregations with a healthy parish life and active ministries of education. What is outlined above is what all congregations strive to *do*. It is part of our reason for being.

A congregation anchored in a faith formation model of ministry, however, can offer children of God like Jane a broader and richer experience of Christ in their lives. The guiding principle in offering additional opportunities for worship and formation is this: anything an adult can find ritually meaningful can be equally inspiring for a child. This understanding grows out of a deep commitment that all are children of God, regardless of age. We all have the capacity for experiences with the holy. In fact, our practices would lead us to believe that formation can often be even *more* inspiring for a child than for an adult. Children can and do experience God richly and fully. Their assent to the holy is instinctive and freely expressed. It is not only intellectual in its origin, but it can be immeasurably valuable in shaping how one thinks about God in the future. We use the language of creating "hooks" in the young Christian mind. These hooks provide a future place for the more complex theological aspects of our faith and tradition to be caught in the mind of the believer. Here are some examples of Jane's getting God in her body through ritual immersion.

From the Sunday after her baptism until this day, Jane has touched the baptismal waters and made the sign of the cross each time she is near the font. Early in her life, her parents did this ritual of remembrance and thanksgiving for her. On their way to communion, either mom or dad would dip her tiny hand into the font and trace a wet cross from her head to her chest, from shoulder to shoulder.

The parish watches enthusiastically and with a healthy, holy curiosity for the day when little ones will reach into those waters for the first time *themselves* and repeat their parents' action. We watch with eager joy as the children eventually come to do this standing on their own two feet, finally tall enough to reach into the baptismal waters on their own. As followers of Jesus, shouldn't we celebrate a child's being tall enough to remember her baptism on her own? It's far more important than being tall enough to ride Splash Mountain, a culturally celebrated milestone. As parish pastors, we try to keep these priorities in perspective.

As she matures, there will never be a time when Jane will not be able to recall the simple, self-affirming ritual of remembering her baptism. She will know that in this community of faith, it is simply what a Christian *does*.

Unfortunately, Jane developed a health crisis. As it does for many children, the day came when she needed to have her tonsils removed. One infection after another was wearing her down and her pediatrician suggested that a tonsillectomy would be an appropriate treatment. Jane's parents had been watching and learning on Sunday mornings in ways that we as their pastors had not been aware. They had seen week after week how the chapel of our congregation's worship space is open for healing prayers during the distribution of communion. In fact, Jane's mom and dad may have availed themselves of this ministry on one occasion or another. But on the Sunday before her surgery, they came with the expectant conviction that this was a fitting ritual for Jane. They believed that the liturgical prayers and anointing that their daughter would receive from her church would be an appropriate complement to the medical treatment she would receive at the hospital. At the hands of her pastor, Jane would know the care of Jesus and the role of Jesus in her healing. The ritual of prayer, which she requested in her own words—not those of her parents—and the anointing with oil laid the groundwork in her young mind and body to receive the physical healing that God had in store for her at the hospital in the week to come.

Having had our eyes opened by Jane and her parents to the possibilities of healing prayers for a youngster, we were moved to action. The very next hour the associate pastor who works closely with our prayer shawl ministry came into Jane's Sunday school class, bringing with her a hand-knit prayer shawl. With her peers laying their hands upon her as the shawl was put into place, Jane received what every adult in the parish receives if we know that they are anticipating surgery: the gift of a shawl, the comfort of the community, the prayers of the faithful. A new, blazing trail had been forged for us all by some of the youngest among us, and we are grateful.

The Faith Formation of Jane

Because Jane's mother, Amy, served the parish as a catechist in The WAY this past year, Jane often accompanied her mom to Sunday evening mealtime. Along with other new and longtime members of the congregation, Jane participated in the weekly fellowship meal and not only observed but also contributed to the growing faith of Jesus' disciples in their conversations, questions, and responses during the dinner hour.

Another place that Jane benefitted from the ministry of her mother was in the parish's food bank. Coming in a child carrier or stroller, Jane was with her mom each time Amy had a monthly shift of preparing food boxes for distribution and handing them out to those in need who came to receive them. As she grew, she was able to assist with loading the boxes ("Jane, can you find the peanut butter and put it in this box for Mommy?"). Her child's welcome was also refreshing for many of the elderly or homeless men and women who came to receive the gift of food.

The culmination of our faith formation process comes in the Lenten season, particularly in Holy Week. The faithful participation of Jane's family in these services and rites has made available to her a further rich and varied palette of possibilities for her growth in grace.

Born in April, Jane did not receive the imposition of ashes on her forehead until she was almost one. It was the following Ash Wednesday that gave her the opportunity to be carried by her parents to the font where the waters that once had blessed her were replaced with the ashes that spoke the hard truth reflected in the words of their imposition: "Remember that you are dust, and to dust you shall return."

As a pastor, there is something particularly jarring about imposing ashes on the forehead of an infant. Their tender skin, their lovely eyes, their fine and wispy hair stand in stark contrast to the Fall-imposed formula that speaks the truth about the human condition. Yet, by including infants and preschool children, elementary through high school kids, and adults in the annual ritual, we speak an often neglected truth about our sinful lives and our need for Christ's forgiveness and healing. Each disciple of Christ stands in need of God's baptismal grace. So, along with her peers young and old, as a baptized child of God, Jane's forehead was etched with ashes.

As Jane has grown in years, Todd and Amy have been extremely faithful to their commitments to bring her to the services of God's house, provide for her instruction in the Christian faith, and place in her hands the Holy Scriptures so that she may lead a godly life until the day of Jesus Christ.[2] With each passing year, Jane has been present for the Maundy Thursday liturgy of confession that includes individual absolution. She has come forward in the long line of worshipers as the Triduum opens to receive the assurance of forgiveness from the very hands that imposed upon her the ashes of mortality calling her to repentance and the keeping of a holy Lent. In our tradition, Maundy Thursday also includes the opportunity for a few of the gathered to have their feet washed as a reminder of Christ's last commandment—the "mandate" or "maundy" from which the liturgical celebration takes its name. Jane was one of the many whose feet were washed as a part of our past year's Maundy Thursday liturgy.

With all of these and the regular rhythm of Sunday and festival worship, Jane has learned to receive God through her senses. She has received the Word of God in her body; she was blessed with formation before she was blessed with *in*formation. That formation will serve her well as her life in Christ continues to mature and grow.

Only God knows what the years ahead will hold for this disciple of Jesus named Jane. In our congregation, as we practice the natural continuation of faith formation that takes place among adults who walk in The WAY, we live in the confidence and hope that *formation* will lay the groundwork for the *information* that is yet to come. Jane is participating in the rituals of washing and remembering, hearing God's Word and being blessed at the table. Her table fellowship with others who are growing in grace and her deep immersion in the rites that comprise a rich and vibrant faith are part of the rhythm of her life. Through them, Jane is having a garden cultivated in her mind, her heart, and her life in which

2. *Lutheran Book of Worship*, 121.

the rich theology of the Christian tradition can take root and grow. There is plenty of time for that growth in the life that stretches out before her. All of the experiences that she has had so far in faith formation have come in her tender years. Jane has just turned four.

4

A New Model for Sunday School

OUR CONGREGATION'S INCREASING emphasis on baptism and faith formation spilled over into our educational ministry and transformed Sunday school. Parents who had their children enrolled in Sunday school were increasingly persons who themselves had come to the parish through The WAY. In addition, many of the teachers themselves had been in The WAY either as a candidate or as a sponsor. Reflecting on Scripture and bringing their own life experiences to these sacred texts changed the emphasis and the direction of the education for children offered on Sunday mornings.

The result was that Sunday school was no longer an arena in which week after week students were offered a particular preplanned lesson with requisite goals and objectives. The classes became much more focused on what questions the students—regardless of age— brought to a biblical text and how they might interact with that text to be formed in faith.

Early on in our journey with The WAY, several members of the parish and the Children and Family Minister were trained in Godly Play.[1] As it turned out, nothing regarding our Sunday school format could have been more Spirit-directed than the institution of this method of faith-forming education for young children. Its core methods and philosophy, along with its thoughtful adaptation

---

1. See http://www.godlyplayfoundation.org/newsite/Main.php.

to our setting by wise and well-trained leaders, have made Godly Play both a gift and a building block in the structure of our life of forming disciples of Jesus.

Godly Play, held on Sunday mornings at 10 A.M. among children, bears a great deal of resemblance to The WAY held on Sunday evenings at 5 P.M. among adults. At its core is a small group "Bible study," a story told and heard, not simply read from a preprinted store-bought curriculum. Through the story-leader's careful teaching and the gift of Godly Play manipulatives,[2] the saving gospel of Jesus as it is revealed in both the Old and the New Testaments resounds in the ears of five-, six-, and seven-year-olds. The children are told a story with the assistance of colorful backdrops, wooden figures representing everything from Noah to the Temple. They listen as God's saving grace unfolds before their eyes and in their ears. Open-ended reflection questions—those "I wonder" starters that fuel the Sunday evening Bible study among adults—cap off the telling of the Bible story.

The children then go on to further experience the story through the next step of instruction. Various stations around the classroom offer children options of their own choosing. A sandpit doubles as a desert in which little fingers help God's people wander toward a promised land. Reminders of previous weeks' stories are accessible for—just as the name implies—*Godly play*. Each child chooses an area in which to explore, guided by their teacher, and both individual or small group exploration and experiences are available.

The beginning and ending rites of a Godly Play Sunday school class bear much resemblance to a Sunday evening session of The WAY as well. Mirroring the meal and welcome hospitality of Sunday evenings, class begins with the children gathering with one another after the early worship service for a light snack and a time of singing. Community is created. Then it's off to small groups to have the Scriptures cracked open as described above. The leader (read: catechist) offers a recap of the day's lesson as each Godly Play class

2. Manipulatives are prepurchased story aids from Godly Play, many of which are beautifully crafted wooden cutouts of Bible characters, Noah's ark, the Temple, and other helpful and significant biblical storytelling props.

session comes to an end. Then, in the most striking similarity to adult catechesis offered in our parish, the children pray with and for one another for the week to come. After a hearty morning of 8:30 worship and 10 o'clock Godly Play, the kids are sent into the world to discover God at work with new ears and eyes.

Most years at the Easter Vigil, the story of Noah and the ark is told in the style of Godly Play by one of the trained and experienced Godly Play instructors. This faithful laywoman captivates the imaginations of the children gathered around her as she lovingly tells the story using her small wooden ark and beautiful dove. And not only the children: she holds the attention of the entire congregation, adults included. You can hear a pin drop. But more importantly, you can feel the Word of God coming to life among us, God's people.

The methods, storytelling, and open-ended questions of Godly Play are much more in concert with the style of formational teaching that takes place among adults in Sunday evening reflection groups at The WAY. Leaving a child to ponder *an* interpretation of a Scripture text rather than *the* interpretation of a Scripture text became much more consistent with what the adults in The WAY were experiencing. While there was no less emphasis on the biblical narrative or its importance in sharing the history of God's activity among God's people, the stories became a tool for creating faith instead of a moral code by which to maintain it. The baptismal motifs of dying and rising, slavery and freedom, forgiveness and new life became the lens through which biblical stories were presented and taught. An example from an older group of post-Godly Play children's instruction will illustrate.

Imagine a class of fifth graders embracing the text of the prodigal son (Luke 15:11–32). Before we began using the Godly Play model in the year 2000, a typical Sunday school lesson in our setting probably would have gone something like this: read the story, consider the characters, imagine who they represent, and ask, "What's the moral of the story?" According to our current model, one of reflection and action, students may encounter the story in a manner more like this: experience the story in several different ways. Listen to it. Listen to a different way of telling it. Act it out.

What are the questions the story raises for you? Who are you most like in this story? To whom do you relate? What can you imagine that God is telling us through this story? Do you see any death and resurrection in it? Who or what died? What did God raise up in its place?

Through a variety of teaching methods—art, music, storytelling, acting, conversation, and reflection—the students encounter biblical texts in this way week after week. There are no class books other than the Bible. There are very few handouts or coloring sheets; any art or project that might arise from class reflection and discussion would be organic rather than prescribed.

Recently, a combined class of third, fourth, and fifth graders decided along with their adult instructors to learn more about the church's ministry to the poor. They agreed on a period of three months to study this topic. The students read and reflected upon appropriate Scripture texts in which Jesus talks about caring for the poor. Then they decided to learn more about how the church in general and our church specifically are helping the poor. The class toured the food bank and heard stories from people they see each week in worship about living out their faith and following Jesus' words by sharing food with those in need. They sent away to our denominational office for information and videos about fair trade and its ministry of offering people a new way of life. Wise adult leaders connected that "new way of life" to resurrection. Their three months culminated in a Fair Trade Bazaar offered to the entire congregation during education hour in which they presented a play that they had written and also sold fair trade goods.

Instead of simply hearing a lesson, the children involved "became" the lesson, responding to the story by touring a food bank, requesting materials from the denomination, acting out a play, and selling fair trade goods. These are fundamental building blocks for a life of faith that will be remembered because they have been *lived*. And as the faith of these young men and women matures, the basic building blocks of action and reflection that this educational model provides will be a foundation upon which they can continue to build an increasingly deep understanding of God's work in the world.

As you may have surmised, in our setting we do not purchase printed curriculum. Our Sunday school, our Wednesday evening elementary age Bible classes, and our confirmation materials are all produced locally, written primarily by those who are teaching the classes at hand, either pastors or skilled and committed laypersons. The Bible story stands at the very center of it all.

Contrary to expectations, this local production of materials is not a daunting task. We have found that for us it is far more rewarding and meaningful in communicating the gospel of Jesus than using materials that were produced hundreds of miles away and many years ago. To be sure, there is a place for curriculum. But the immediacy, the application, and the relevance of material that is tailored to the local congregational situation are faith formational. By having a hand in developing what topics will be encountered and how they will be experienced, the students gain a new level of investment in the learning process. It is one thing to read or tell a Bible story in which Jesus says, "Love one another." It is quite a different educational experience to have that text elaborated through the inclusion of a story written about a little girl their age who lives in Africa and who almost died of malaria because she didn't have a mosquito net; to create a bulletin board that shares information about the denomination's malaria campaign; and to have the students organize an offering for the congregation to buy a certain number of mosquito nets for their peers across the ocean. It is a formational approach built upon action in the name of Jesus rather than answers about him. *That* is baptismal living.

5

Confirmation Ministry

As with Sunday school, we began to see that our baptismal ministries for adults and those for young adults preparing to affirm their baptisms through the rite of confirmation were in need of a closer connection. In our liturgies, the rites involved were exactly the same. Yet the process for youth was still all about *information*, while the shift to *formation* had been made in our walk with adults. Why was it that those in our confirmation ministry—typically thirteen- or fourteen-year-olds—were still being prepared to be baptized or to affirm their baptisms using a model that emphasized *information*?

Not surprisingly, it was one of the confirmation students who pointed out the difference to us. She asked the completely reasonable question, after watching several years of adult formation and the candidates' affirmations at the Vigil of Easter, "Why is it that kids have to do stuff around here to affirm their baptisms that you would never expect or ask an adult to do?" Good question.

While we in pastoral leadership were beginning to see the discrepancy for ourselves, our young student's question focused the challenge and began moving us in a new direction.

Our first step was to address the "graduation" aspect of confirmation ministry—the not-so-mysterious disappearance of young people from the church following their confirmation day. Just when we had brought them to the point of affirming their faith, we seemed to excuse them from it. They were gone and we acted helpless. It always felt so disappointing to lose them just when their lives had been so richly immersed in formation. To address this, we both lowered and raised the age of confirmation ministry instruction and changed the rite of confirmation to the early autumn.

By beginning confirmation ministry in late elementary school, we had the opportunity as pastors to begin to connect with the religious imagination of our students at an earlier age. Building on the work that had already been routine for them in worship, Sunday school, and choir, the sixth graders meet with a pastor each week for half an hour as part of a larger Wednesday evening ministry program that we call Bread for the Journey. The curriculum for this rich half hour is straightforward, as are the goals. By sharing a read-aloud story together, our goal is to begin to show developing minds that God is at work not only in the church and in their individual lives but in the world as well. Stories are chosen that reinforce this theology. The stories range from O. Henry's "The Gift of the Magi" to Walt Wangerin's "Ragman" to Dr. Seuss's "The Sneetches." A smattering of Bible stories is included as well—the prodigal son; the two brothers, one who says yes and one who says no; and the Christmas story from Luke 2, to name a few. A complete annual catalog is included in Appendix 1. The class "checks in" with one another by sharing that day's highs and lows, which builds a sense of community and the shared plight of sixth grade life. We light a candle, say a prayer, and then a pastor reads that week's story aloud. Perhaps a few "I wonder" questions—borrowed from Godly Play—are asked at the end, but the usual routine is to allow the story to speak for itself.

Pondering "I wonder" questions offers the students an opportunity to reflect without necessarily placing them in the position of having to answer a question "correctly" or "incorrectly." In O. Henry's "The Gift of the Magi," for example, one might draw students into the conversation in the way illustrated by example A below, rather than example B.

Example A: "I wonder what Jim was feeling as he walked into the flat and saw that Della's hair had been cut?"

Example B: "What was Jim feeling when he saw that Della had cut her hair?"

The first example builds a strong foundation for asking more complex questions about God, faith, Jesus, and a host of other confirmation topics that will be discussed in later years of formation. The students are trained in such a way to be more reflective and less reflexive in immediately lunging toward the "right" answer.

Another important by-product of the time spent together in storytelling is the opportunity to have the pastoral staff connect more directly to students of this age. It also helps us as pastors and staff tune their ears for the "faith that comes from hearing" (Rom 10:17) in these, their maturing years.

Our seventh-grade year, while based on that Lutheran mainstay, *Luther's Small Catechism*, approaches the text in a way that is more experiential than it had been prior to our becoming a faith formation congregation. Using methods similar to those discussed above, the instructors and students together walk through the various aspects of the Catechism's contents. One of the chief goals is to have the words of the creed, the Ten Commandments, and the Lord's Prayer come to life in the everyday experiences of seventh graders. While we find memorizing parts of these treasures of the faith as well as Luther's explanations of them helpful, it is a greater goal to help students find applications for them in their middle school lives. *Why do these words matter?*

An illustration is in order. In his explanation of the eighth commandment, "You shall not bear false witness against your neighbor," Luther writes:

> What does this mean?
>
> Answer: We should fear and love God, and so we should not tell lies about our neighbors, nor betray, slander, or defame them, but should apologize for them, speak well of them, and interpret charitably all that they do.[1]

Thinking about this commandment from a faith formation perspective, and considering the developmental stage of a seventh grader,

1. Luther, *Small Catechism*, in *The Book of Concord*, 343.

a great way to begin the conversation would be to say, "*I wonder if anyone has ever said or done anything* to you *that has destroyed your reputation?*" The responses will be immediate and plentiful, guaranteed. Go deeper: "*Has anyone ever done this to you in a way that made you want to strike back in the same way? What does this commandment say to us about that?*"

By tying the ancient words of God's exodus people to an experience earlier that day in middle school, the wise instructor is helping the student be molded and shaped in an ancient faith that is coming to life through the power of a living word. This is baptismal teaching. It has been our experience that sometimes the "aha moments" are so strong, deep, and profound that they actually feel like crashing waters.

To continue the eighth commandment lesson, one might move into a conversation about how difficult it is to speak well of someone who has been or is being hurtful or slanderous to you. It is also a great opportunity to reflect back upon and draw illustrations from the rich treasury of shared stories to which the students were exposed in sixth grade. When, for whatever reason, the students are slow to share their own life experiences, having those of fictional characters upon which to draw as a shared vocabulary is a rich resource.

PARTNERSHIP IN MINISTRY: CONFIRMATION MENTORS

One of the hallmarks of baptismal theology that our practice of The WAY has helped us see in a new light is the public nature of the baptismal covenant. Every baptism takes place at public worship, because every baptism is a public act and involves not only the newly baptized and their parent(s) or sponsor(s), but the entire community of faith. When a child is baptized, the congregation responds with these or similar words: "We welcome you into the body of Christ and the mission we share: join us in giving thanks and praise to God and bearing God's creative and redeeming word to all the world."[2]

2. *Lutheran Book of Worship*, 125.

One of the ways in which our congregation lives out this partnership is by matching each student in confirmation ministry with an adult mentor. The task of the mentor is similar to that of a sponsor with an adult candidate in The WAY: to be a companion on the journey. We invite a few suggestions from the students about who they might like to have as their mentor, but ultimately the pastors make the assignment based on what we believe will be the strongest match for each student's faith development.

While there is a formal meeting time between student and mentor once each month during the Christian Education hour, it's not unusual for much more lively and frequent connections to occur between the pair at other times. They sometimes worship together. They share time in line by the latte cart on Sunday mornings. They share birthday greetings and exchange e-mails. They do what Christian friends *do*—they walk together in a journey of faith. Although this should not surprise us, the mentors grow in their faith as they walk side by side with young men and women preparing to affirm. We see it and expect it in The WAY. We see it in confirmation ministry as well and are growing to expect it there, too. What a baptismal gift of circular faith.

PREPARING TO AFFIRM

In our particular faith tradition, when an infant is baptized, parents and sponsors take on the promises of the faith on his or her behalf. When young adults have been instructed and are prepared to take on those promises for themselves, they participate in a rite that is called interchangeably Affirmation of Baptism or confirmation. At the time of the public rite, these are the promises that a young man or woman of faith affirms:

> I intend to continue in the covenant God made with me
> in holy baptism:
> > to live among God's faithful people,
> > to hear the word of God and share in the Lord's supper,
> > to proclaim the good news of God in Christ through
> > word and deed,

to serve all people, following the example of Jesus,
and to strive for justice and peace in all the earth.[3]

The eighth grade fall semester leading up to the day of Affirmation of Baptism in worship is, without a doubt, my favorite part of the confirmation ministry journey. The individual promises above are explored in a case study. This homegrown curriculum, called "Preparing to Affirm," translates the liturgical rite into real-life application of each affirmation. The question that Luther poses over and over again in the *Small Catechism*—"What does this mean?"—becomes the question that we explore with each of these soon-to-be affirmed promises. The case studies that we've prepared to explore each of the six commitments of the affirmation of baptism liturgy can be found in Appendix 2. They form the core of the September and October Wednesday night confirmation curriculum leading up to the affirmation of baptism liturgy on the final Sunday of October.

While these weekly case studies are the substance of class discussion in Preparing to Affirm, the work of preparing an individual statement of faith is an additional task explored by each student, the pastor, parents, and confirmation mentor.

The statements of faith are as unique as the students themselves. A few sentences plucked from several students' statements over the years will serve to illustrate. Amelia chose to model her statement of faith on the framework of the promises of the affirmation of baptism liturgy. Here is what she had to say about service to others in Jesus' name.

> *To serve all people, following the example of our Lord Jesus.* Jesus didn't just preach to a certain group of people. He didn't heal just Jews. He didn't dine with just priests. Jesus showed that he cared for all. He blessed children. He preached to the unfaithful. He healed sinners. He dined with both women and men. If Jesus can be so open and caring, then we can do our small part to help everyone. Whether it is working at a soup kitchen, reading to and playing with little children, visiting the sick

3. *Evangelical Lutheran Worship*, 237.

or chatting with the elderly, we can all do something to serve someone else.

—Amelia Mockett, 2005

Liam, whose statement is shown here in its entirety, chose to focus on the communal aspect of being a child of God and the sense of acceptance that he has come to feel through the congregation's ministry.

> When we go to church as a family, we all get equal seats. John [Liam's brother] and I don't argue over the best one because in church all the pews are the same. It makes me feel welcomed in the church community.
>
> When I move out from our Moody family pew, I see everyone sitting in the same kind of pews as we are. This tells me that at church there is no popular group or nerdy group. There is no in-between group. Everyone is equal in God's eyes.
>
> To me, God is everything good. God loves everybody. God doesn't turn anybody away from faith. When I think of God, I feel accepted. The other people at church are accepted, too. This tells me that God accepts everybody.
>
> When I go to church, God is not the only one who accepts me. I feel like the whole congregation accepts me for who I am. This means that I don't have to meet their expectations. I can act like the person that God created me to be. At school, you sometimes dress or act the way others do to be more popular. But at church, you can dress and act like who you really are—a child of God.

—Liam Moody, 2011

Liam's words are echoed a year later in Jonathan's statement of faith. Their shared sense of community in Christ is an attribute of a formational congregation that spans the generations and unites all God's people.

> When I began singing with the youth choir and Valerie, our director, I felt that this was more than just a choir, it was one big community that stood up for each other. We all came from different places and had different interests. Yet we are all able to get along and be friends. This is the exact same thing as church. When we all first come to

church we don't know what to expect, but then we all leave knowing each other and feeling safe.

—Jonathan Maier, 2012

The statements are published in the worship bulletin on the Sunday of Affirmation of Baptism and also posted on the main bulletin board in the narthex along with a baptismal picture and a current picture of each student. This is a very big deal. The congregation anticipates the posting of these statements each year, and one can take great joy in watching adult members flock to the bulletin board to see the pictures and read the statements. Students know from parish tradition that their faith is important to the congregation.

CONTINUING CONFIRMATION

Many parishes and parish leaders lament the loss of their young men and women following confirmation. Yet few of us take intentional steps to assure their ongoing connection to the life of the parish. One of the ways that happens in our setting is through the continuing interest and friendship of the confirmation mentor. Another is through the active involvement of almost every young person in our Youth Choir ministry. But the most effective way that we have found to cement young men and women into the life of the parish is continuing confirmation instruction. Their classes do not end the week after the liturgy of Affirmation of Baptism on the last Sunday of October.

For their very first post-affirmation of baptism class, the eighth graders—their faces still shining with anointing oil from the previous Sunday's confirmation rite—meet with and become the instructors for the seventh graders. The goals are simple:

1. place the eighth graders in the position of being bearers of the faith and tradition for the next generation, their seventh grade colleagues;

2. give them an opportunity to reflect upon and teach the power of the past Sunday's rite;

3. immediately keep them in the pattern of coming to class.

The sorts of conversations that usually transpire in this session include comments such as these:

> "It [the service of affirmation of baptism] is a really big deal and you should take it seriously."
>
> "I wish I had taken more time in preparing my statement of faith and put more thought into it."
>
> "You should pay attention in class. This stuff is important."
>
> "When the pastor says 'memory verse,' he means 'MEMORY verse.'"

They will have the opportunity to live much of their own advice, for the following week they are right back into a new class, made up of eighth through twelfth graders who, together with a lay instructor, continue the journey through the questions of faith.

We are blessed in the Lutheran tradition to have such a rich and Spirit-filled understanding of holy baptism. It helps us see that while the day of baptism itself is an essential moment of joy and transformation in the life of every Christian, the gift—or the responsibility—does not stop then. Luther encourages us to return to our baptismal covenant each and every day. He points us to the gift of awaking every morning, refreshed and renewed in the promises God made with us in holy baptism. He teaches us to make the sign of the cross and remember this promise from the *Small Catechism*:

> Baptism signifies that the old person in us with all sins and evil desires is to be drowned and die through daily sorrow for sin and through repentance, and on the other hand that daily a new person is to come forth and rise up to live before God in righteousness and purity forever.[4]

I like to think of it as being born again and again and again and again and again. . . . And I like to teach it that way, too: living water, ebbing and flowing from the baptismal font all the way into each of our lives and, in this case, into the lives of wonderful, surprising, faithful women and men in middle school and beyond. These are waters through which we pass again and again and again and again . . .

4. Luther, *Small Catechism*, in *The Book of Concord*, 349.

6

Pre-Marital Counseling

IMAGINE THIS SETTING: the room is small, and three persons are gathered together around a table. On the center of the table are an unlit candle and three Bibles. Some other papers lie off to one side. There are words of welcome and greeting. Then an invocation is spoken, the candle is lighted, and one of the three, the pastor, prays aloud in words similar to these: "Gracious and loving God, as you have promised, we know that your Spirit is with us. Help us in our time together to be aware of that Spirit, and through its power may your Word be alive in us. Amen."

One of the first areas of ministry to become influenced and therefore changed as a result of our being a faith formation congregation was our ministry of pre-marital counseling.

For the first two-thirds of my ministry, work in this area was highly influenced by the PREPARE/ENRICH inventory,[1] a staple of ministry for many, if not most, Lutheran pastors. This extremely helpful assessment of a couple's strengths and growth areas provides rich fodder for pre-marital conversation and exploration. Even its language of strengths and growth areas as opposed to strengths and weaknesses is helpful and instructive. I have found it to be a wonderful tool, and I continue to use it. But I've also found that with faith formation as the scaffolding upon which all of ministry

---

1. See https://www.prepare-enrich.com

is built, the Church can offer more of its unique gifts to couples planning to marry.

Many of our couples are with us as a result of requesting a wedding in our beautiful space. Lovely churches with long aisles and deeply colored carpet are appealing, even to couples who are not at all familiar with the church and its work in the world. Our approach to such non-member weddings is to invite the couple to worship, at which time an appointment for a face-to-face conversation between pastor and couple can be arranged.

The theme of that conversation is this: *we are much more interested in your marriage than we are in your wedding.* In other words, if you're merely looking for a venue, then this may not be the place for you. However, if you're looking for a place where your marriage can be grounded, for a community that can offer you support over the long haul of your lives together, and for a place where you can avail yourselves of the gifts that God has for you to strengthen and sustain this relationship, then you've probably come to the right place. If the latter is the case, then the couple is enrolled in both pre-marital counseling and in The WAY. If they choose not to make a commitment to this faith community, then we invite them to continue to worship with us but suggest that they look elsewhere for a place to celebrate their wedding.

A NEW MODEL
FOR PRE-MARITAL COUNSELING

Here's what we began to notice. In the former model, as the couple's pre-marital counseling was taking place alongside their baptismal preparation in The WAY, the two processes bore little resemblance to one another. Couples who were highly engaged in scriptural reflection in small groups on Sunday evenings were being counseled in a highly psycho-emotive model on Monday evening when they came to the office for pre-marital counseling. It was not a matter of abandoning the great work and thoughtful preparation that a tool such as PREPARE/ENRICH can provide. It was rather a matter of supplementing it with the great discoveries that we were experiencing through faith formation in other arenas of congregational life.

Our first step was to think baptismally. It took a while for us to see that the riches of the living Word, Jesus Christ, fully present in the living waters, are not confined to the rites directly related to baptism. In fact, that living Word, Jesus, fully immersed in the baptismal waters, cannot—will not—be contained. For work with those planning to marry, this meant we wanted to have the scriptural story spill out of the font and take central place at the counseling table. It meant that we were called to bring the Word that is alive in the font to life around the counseling table in the office.

A complete template for doing this style of pre-marital counseling is laid out in Appendix 3. The remainder of this chapter will offer an overview of how such a method is influenced by adult catechesis and why that is important to the couple's formation as a "church of two."

The work of Paul Bauermeister was highly influential in forming my theology of Christian marriage. In an incisive article published in *Currents in Mission and Theology* in 1983,[2] Bauermeister lays out the different roles that partners play in one another's lives, each new role increasing in its level of intimacy. What is so absolutely compelling about the article is that it points out that in Christian marriage, the highest level of intimacy is not sexual but spiritual. As a couple moves beyond the role of lovers and into the role of priests for one another, they are able to experience the transformative power of God's love in their lives at a level not often imagined or explored. This is a baptismal model of living together as a couple within the larger community of faith, drawing from that community joy in times of prosperity and sustenance in times of suffering.

The unspoken goals of pre-marital counseling had previously been assisting couples to understand their values and patterns of thinking around such topics as finances, conflict resolution, role relationships, and the like. Moving to a faith formation model of counseling that took Bauermeister's work more seriously afforded

---

2. Bauermeister, "Anatomy of Intimacy."

the opportunity for couples to receive two primary gifts of intimacy from the church as the first tier of their marriage preparation: Scripture and prayer. It is not that the former goals were abandoned in favor of the latter. It was rather that Scripture and prayer were now the roads into a deeper understanding and appreciation of the various aspects of a marital relationship. Said another way, the couple has the opportunity to discover how Scripture, prayer, worship, service, and community are means by which a marriage can be strengthened and upheld. It makes incarnate what we often say in the church about marriage, but seldom teach: *marriage is not the private possession of the couple alone. A marriage belongs to and is set within the community of faith.*

Because the couple participates simultaneously in pre-marital counseling and The WAY, they begin to imagine and experience firsthand how their marriage will be upheld and supported by the larger community. The questions they discuss with the pastor spark questions that they bring to the small group. Members of their small group pray for them as each Sunday evening's Bible study ends. They have the confidence and the support of knowing that their small group is praying for them throughout the coming week.

As both counseling and study are a steady part of the couple's preparation on the way to a marriage commitment, so is weekly worship. Since everything that is discussed in Sunday evening study is drawn from Sunday morning worship—particularly scriptural stories and the sermon—the couple is now also developing the pattern of weekly worship. They are learning, perhaps for the first time (or perhaps for the first time as adults), of the church's mission in the world. Poised as they are for a lifetime of commitment to one another, they hear the words of the sermon and pray the prayers of the church and sing its hymns of praise and petition with different ears. All the gifts God offers work together to form a communal setting in which they are preparing for a lifetime of commitment. No longer is their pre-marital counseling a private endeavor isolated in the pastor's office. They are people of God set in the community of God. It is with these men and women next to whom they worship and pray, sing and share, eat and drink, that they will find strength for the challenges and joys that lie ahead of them as partners in marriage.

Recently, a couple who had completed their pre-marital counseling, gone through the previous year's cycle of The WAY, and affirmed their baptism at the Easter Vigil found that they were having some difficulties and questions as their August marriage approached. Rather than speak to the pastors, they talked with their WAY sponsors and catechist. Without the awareness or involvement of either pastor, their WAY small group from the prior year reconvened in the summer months to offer them support and prayer. There it was—the baptismal water from the Easter Vigil splitting open once again for two of God's contemporary people to walk from slavery to freedom at the hand of their WAY group, just as God's people had walked to freedom at the hand of Moses long ago.

PRACTICING PRAYER

Where else, if not in pre-martial counseling, will a couple learn *together* to pray with and for one another? Ideally, of course, this would be a spiritual discipline that each partner brings to the marriage and, as easily as they blend their finances or their bodies, they would blend their individual lives of conversation with God. This has not been my experience. They are being formed as disciples in The WAY. That formation can carry over to and be supplemented in their formation as a couple through forming shared spiritual disciplines and practices.

So, one goal of a fifty-minute session together is to provide an arena and some tools for prayer. *How* does a couple do this? *Why* would a couple do this? One way is to introduce a simple, straightforward, and honest communication with our Creator. The counselor or pastor can do this at the start of the session, giving an idea of how a prayer might be offered. The couple can then be invited to offer a closing prayer of gratitude and praise as the session comes to an end. The goal is not to have the couple emulate the pastor's style or even his or her language. The goal is simply to have it happen.

If it is not happening in the safety of the pastor's office where it is encouraged, nurtured, and coached, one can certainly assume that it is probably not happening elsewhere in the couple's life together.

DISCOVERING THE RICHES OF SCRIPTURE

The same sort of coaching is important in the couple's exploration of Scripture. We who lead in churches continually remind our parishioners that reading the Bible is a great idea; what we seldom provide, however, at least in my experience, is the *how*. *How* would one go about reading the Bible—as an individual or a couple—unless someone offers instruction? It is a question as old and familiar as this one from the book of Acts: "Philip asked [the Ethiopian], 'Do you understand what you are reading?' He replied, 'How can I unless someone guides me?'" (Acts 8:30–31).

It seems so basic and fundamental to our lives of faith in the church that to see it written down is almost embarrassing. Yet outside the evangelical traditions, I know of very few models for training Christians—either new or well-seasoned ones—for the fundamental task of reading, understanding, and applying Scripture to life. This is the underlying premise of the catechumenal model, applied not only to pre-marital preparations but to all of life: God speaks to us through Scripture. The Bible is a living Word. It *does* apply to our lives today, here and now. We are immeasurably enriched by its presence in and application to our lives in every aspect. What is incumbent upon the leadership of the church to provide is the *how*. How do we use the Bible? How can it speak? How does God work through it in our lives? In the present conversation, the question is more specific: how can the Scriptures speak to us in this intense and wonderful time of preparation for spending our lives together as a husband and a wife?

A certain couple, one a lifelong Lutheran and the other new to the Christian faith outside of its cultural manifestations, hear the following, from John 15: "I am the vine, you are the branches. . . . Love one another as I have loved you."

In a usual session the entire passage is read, slowly and intentionally, by the pastor, as the couple follows along, each with their own Bible. The standard pastoral question for reflection on these words opens the conversation: "How do you imagine that God is speaking to you through these words of Scripture about your relationship with one another?" And they're off!

She imagines how difficult it will be to continually love Ray as she has experienced God loving her. "How does one do that?" she muses aloud. "Try harder?"

He, meanwhile, is caught up by the image of the dead branches being cut off, cast into the fire and burned. He begins to wonder what parts of his old life will be left behind—"forsaking all others"—to commit exclusively to *this* relationship.

Can you imagine the rich fodder for discussion that has already been placed on the table from these initial, varying responses to the reading? *And* they have come at the Holy Spirit's prompting from the Scriptures themselves. The Bible has primacy in this pre-marital counseling model as the book of faith, the book of life, and relationship formation. The rich and time-tested tools of an inventory such as PREPARE/ENRICH now emerge as supporting sources rather than as the primary source.

A counselor/pastor can now wisely take the couple's initial responses to the Scripture reading and direct them toward a richer understanding of their strengths and growth areas.

"How does one do that?" one of them asks. The "that" in their question is *love one another as I have loved you.*

A plethora of reflections, reinforced by their work with the PREPARE/ENRICH inventory, emerge as possible trajectories of the conversation. The pastor might prompt the couple with a question or statement:

> How has love been shared in your families of origin?
>
> How do those models ground each of you in a self-giving love?
>
> What have your experiences as a couple of such sacrificial love been so far?
>
> Share an example with one another of a time when you felt loved by your partner unconditionally.

GROUNDED IN BAPTISM

I'll say it again: the wonder of this strategy for counseling couples on their way to the altar is that it is grounded in the Scriptures and reinforced with prayer. Both of these tools are the unique possession of the church. Not only is the couple being exposed to the helpful tools of personality or family systems analysis and psycho-emotive wisdom, but these great gifts for relationship now have an anchor in their life of faith.

As the couple prepares in the pastor's office for an upcoming marriage and also prepares in a small group Bible study group with The WAY, each process complements the other. Since they are preparing for baptism or its affirmation in their Sunday evening small groups, they come to pre-marital counseling immersed in baptismal theology. The images and metaphors of dying and rising make sense. Through this scripturally centered approach to their couples' counseling, they are doubly blessed. In both gifts that the church offers them *and* at weekly worship, they are grounded in the Word of God, in the waters of baptism, in the death and resurrection of Christ.

7

Hospitality and Welcome

To be sure, *hospitality* and *welcome* are difficult terms to define, and even more difficult practices to live into as a community of faith. The natural excitement and joy of gathering with people we know and who share our faith can be a wonderful thing. Unfortunately, it can also quickly close out those new to faith as well as those looking to renew a life of faith in a new community of believers. The joy of a fellowship community can be easily interpreted by visitors as a sense of closed cliquishness that confirms the perception that Christians have difficulty welcoming the newcomer.

Pastors and parish leaders are in a key position to model hospitality and welcome. We find that being vested prior to liturgy and being available in the narthex for twenty to thirty minutes prior to the service offers a great opportunity to model welcome. Not only are we as liturgical leaders able to welcome those of the regular worshiping congregation back to the house of God, but we can also identify newcomers, offer them a first welcome, and, where necessary and desirable, connect them with other members of the Sunday assembly. It's a bit of a balancing act. Many persons who visit congregations, especially in a secular city such as Seattle, prefer to travel under the radar. A pastoral sensitivity to the desires of the newcomer is an essential tool in providing a genuine welcome. Sometimes that welcome means creating space and not overwhelming the visitor.

This brings us to the larger topic of identifying and highlighting newcomers within the assembly. For a person who is at the very early stages of exploring a life of faith, the desire to be anonymous is paramount. Many well-intentioned parish customs for recognizing visitors often alienate them instead. To be a new person in a new place and to find oneself on uncertain ground both theologically and socially is probably enough of a challenge for a Sunday morning. To single out a visitor by insisting she wear a name tag, or by pinning on her a corsage, or by introducing her in worship often sends her out the door, never to return. A more hospitable welcome is a one-to-one conversation before or after worship that conveys genuine interest and warmth. "Are you visiting us today?" you might say. "We welcome you." Or "Let me know if you have any questions." Or "We hope you'll join us again."

Name tags in and of themselves, though wildly popular, are not helpful in creating an atmosphere of hospitality. Name tags are for business meetings. In a place where the central theology of baptism says that we are all called by the common name "Christian," it is counterproductive to sort people out by name. Pauls speaks of our common identity when he says, "There is no longer Jew or Greek, there is no longer slave or free, there is no longer male and female, for all of you are one in Christ" (Gal 3:28). In the most common scenarios, name tags also immediately distinguish insiders from outsiders. Members have them. Guests do not. Moreover, if everyone has identical stick-on name tags, the act of having one placed upon you, or being asked to wear one, can feel so invasive as to be off-putting rather than welcoming.

This is not to say that names are not important. They are. But an authentic interest in getting to know someone by name is far more hospitable than accomplishing the task of assigning them a tag. We believe names to be so important, in fact, that we make an effort as pastors to learn the names of the newcomers in the narthex so that we can connect that welcoming hospitality with the hospitality of the Lord's table, where the first-time visitor is offered the sacrament by name: "Cheryl, the body of Christ given for you." Almost without exception, new participants in The WAY cite the example of being called by name early in their time among us as one of the most powerful spiritual experiences of visiting our congregation. They also identify this sense of being known and belonging *to God* as one of the reasons they returned. Of course, any hospitality that we extend is hospitality already shared with us by Christ himself: "Very truly, I tell you, whoever receives one whom I send receives me" (John 13:20).

Many parishioners and pastors say, "I just can't remember names. I really need those name tags." Yes, it's true, names are difficult to remember. But as with any spiritual practice, to wean ourselves away from tags and begin a journey of true recognition and welcome is worthy of our time and effort. It's a spiritual *practice*. So it takes practice.

Creating an environment in which people can get to know one another more deeply—whether newcomer or longtime participant—is another key ingredient of hospitality and welcome. Many years ago we noticed that while we were offering coffee between services and a warm environment for conversation and conviviality, many, if not most, members were hastily leaving the early service—perhaps dropping off their children at Sunday school first—and retreating to one of the dozen or so coffee shops within walking distance of the church. Was it really reasonable for us to expect that on Sunday mornings Seattleites, for whom exceptional coffee is a staple six days a week, would be content to drink badly brewed decaf coffee from an aluminum urn? Investing in a parish latte cart solved the problem.

We have barista training just as we have assisting minister training. We put fair trade coffee in the grinder and make it available for purchase by the pound. There's no charge for a latte, but a donation is welcome. All proceeds from the cart are passed on to the world hunger appeal. Kids love getting a steamed milk or a hot chocolate after worship and on their way to Sunday school. Coffee is everywhere in Seattle, so having coffee in the sanctuary during worship is not only permitted but—as we love to say—"expected."

The drain away from adult forum classes and into the streets in search of coffee has been stemmed. There is no better place to get to know a newcomer by name than in the coffee line. It feels as natural as a visit to any coffee shop on any weekday. Yet here the topic of faith is a welcome conversation-starter.

Hospitality is a key ingredient in the Sunday evening gatherings of The WAY as well. A well-cooked, nutritious meal with a vegetarian option is the mainstay. Meals are served buffet or family style at round tables of eight where conversation is easy to join and maintain. This makes for a warm welcome, especially on a dark and dreary Sunday evening in Seattle. Professional childcare is provided by the same persons who offer it on Sunday mornings during worship. Parents can join in the activities of their small group Bible study with the confidence of knowing that their children are in a safe and nurturing environment.

The respectful welcome of children is another key aspect of a parish's ministry of hospitality. Whenever I hear people in various congregations talk about their goals, "bring in more young people" is almost always one of the top three. Yet the prevailing ethos in worship is often one in which young families have a difficult time engaging. The cries of babies, the wiggles of toddlers, the scribbles of second graders and the alleged inattention of middle schoolers are often met with disdain, both spoken and unspoken.

In our setting, children are both welcome and expected to attend worship in its entirety. We believe that worship is for the whole people of God and we practice it as such. Some basic practices make children's presence and participation an identifying characteristic of who we are as God's people.

Pastoral leadership is absolutely key in setting the tone for the welcome and full participation of children. We have worked hard to clarify the expectation and practice that children gather with the assembly as full participants for the entire service. We have also resisted the temptation to conduct Sunday school at the same time as worship, a practice so often justified as "absolutely necessary" for today's busy families. Instruction in and interpretation of worship practices so that children can more fully engage is a regular ingredient of choral instruction, Sunday school, Wednesday evening education, and confirmation ministry. Early communion is the norm. Children's Word is an anticipated ingredient of almost every liturgy. An effort is made to include at least one hymn each week that is accessible to children. Such a hymn would be one that has a refrain, is robust and frequently used in the congregation, or has language that is easily understood by children. An additional element of welcome for the young people in our parish is that the pastors know our kids and welcome them freely and richly.

In helping create a welcoming atmosphere in a congregation that is not used to children, or in one where their presence is considered a "distraction," the attitudes of the pastor and parish leadership are pivotal. Saying "listen to the joyful cries of praise God's children are lifting this morning" can do wonders to set a positive tone. Much better, for example, than "I'll speak louder so you can hear over the crying."

We encourage and expect families with small children to sit near the front, making it easier for children to see and mimic liturgical actions. Children are included as lectors, assisting ministers, cantors, ushers, and choral leaders. A choir of thirty to fifty children takes its place in the choral lineup as liturgical leaders of worship alongside a youth choir and three adult choirs. Each choir enjoys equal status, and all choirs—children, youth, gospel, and chancel—participate and lead worship in a meaningful way when it's their turn.

Rather than a worship attendance card or a communion card that registers attendance, we use a "Count Me In" form as a part of our weekly worship bulletin. The name itself moves away from the corporate model and into the life of Christian community. The main purpose of the form is to allow congregational members to sign up for coming activities and to volunteer for a variety of congregational ministries. Food bank volunteers are recruited, congregational meeting attendance is encouraged, opportunities to be included in parish mailings and e-mailings are offered, and—almost as a side benefit—names, addresses, and e-mails are gathered.

To those first-time visitors who offer an address or an e-mail, a pastor writes a personal note of welcome on Monday. No pressure, just a welcome like the one below.

Dear John and Mary:

We're so glad you visited with us at worship yesterday.
Your presence with us made worship a richer experience
for all of us.

If you have any questions about our congregation and
its ministry, please feel free to be in touch with me at the
addresses or numbers below.

We hope that you'll soon be able to join us again for
worship.

In Christ,

Pastor Paul Hoffman

An office volunteer sends this welcome out by e-mail, or if it is going through the USPO, I write it and mail it myself. It's not daunting. Once in place, it's a simple five-minute task every Monday, yet
it makes all the difference in the world. St. Paul encourages us in
this way: "Contribute to the needs of the saints, extend hospitality
to strangers" (Rom 12:13). Such a tangible welcome is but one way
to shape one's pastoral ministry by biblical practice.

"Is all this really so important?" one might ask. What's so important about offering a welcome to people who don't always know
what they're looking for? Why extend hospitality to those who may
truly want to remain anonymous and who may be put off by too
much attention coming their way? Why strive for something so
hard to define and even harder to put into practice? It is important
because the Scriptures suggest to us in a deep and profound way
that this is really how God's people are called to live with one another: "Let love be genuine" (Rom 12:9). As this chapter comes to
an end, I offer a story of hospitality offered to me that I have never
forgotten. It was—and remains—a moment of true transformation.

While attending a continuing education event at the National
Cathedral in Washington DC more than ten years ago, I found myself at an unusually low spiritual ebb. The materials I found lying
around in the beautiful housing that we were offered next door to
the cathedral pointed me toward an early morning Eucharist in the
great cathedral's undercroft. At the conclusion, the priest offered

the few of us in attendance an opportunity for individual healing prayers at the altar railing, should any of us desire such a rite. Having offered this to others so many times myself, I was well aware of what to expect from such a rite and wondered whether or not this was a good opportunity for me to avail myself of such a rich and gracious gift. That I was even contemplating it was convincing enough. I fell to my knees and waited for the deacon to come to offer prayer and anointing. The deacon asked simply, "For what would you like me to pray?" I felt as I had often imagined Bartimaeus must have felt when kneeling at the feet of Jesus, who asked him, "What would you like me to do for you?"

As his hands dipped into the warm, fragrant oil and were laid upon my head, the most amazing thing happened. I suddenly felt—gently but firmly, from behind me—an additional set of hands, one laid on each of my shoulders. For a moment I thought I was imagining it. Then I imagined that an angel had laid hands on me. And finally, I realized that the "angel" was another person, a welcoming and healing presence that I could never have asked for or imagined. But that was the most welcome and inviting moment I had experienced for a long, long time. "Welcome one another, therefore, just as Christ has welcomed you" (Rom 15:7). I was welcomed. I was healed. Truly touched by living hands, as if by the hands of Christ.

The caring congregation of the cathedral community had provided a place to hear the word and receive the sacrament early on a weekday morning. They had provided a priest to offer those gifts, even though they were well aware that only a handful of us would gather there. Yet these were the same servants of God who ministered to thousands on Sunday mornings and other occasions a few floors above in the main sanctuary. There was candlelight and fragrant oil, generous bread, a spoken word and wine that warmed me as I received it from the common cup. And then there was the assisting minister whose hands embraced my shoulders—the angel who got out of bed early that morning in Washington DC, not knowing who, if anyone, might need her gentle touch, but convinced that in the offering, God's work would be done.

In much the same way, people come to worship week in and week out seeking something of which they are not quite certain. But they will recognize the presence of Christ—the genuine, healing, welcoming presence of Christ—as we offer it as best as our gifts allow in an intentional and thoughtful way. God's people deserve such a welcome. God's people are called to offer such a welcome, one to another. In these offerings of ourselves to others, we sprinkle them with the waters of our own baptism and invite them to a shared baptism in Christ. We live into our vocation. Waters ebb and waters flow, waters that are teeming with Christ.

8

Parish Meetings

FOLLOWING THE MODEL of the burgeoning and successful businesses of the 1950s, sixty years ago many congregations began organizing themselves on the same sort of corporate model. There was an elected board of directors under which, in the best of circumstances, various committees completed tasks to maintain the vision set by the board. In the church, we often called those boards "church councils," "vestries," or "sessions." The prevailing guiding documents were carefully scripted constitutions and *Robert's Rules of Order*.

For many years, in many congregations, in a variety of circumstances, this model of leadership worked wonders. Through it the mission of the gospel was advanced, buildings were built and maintained, outreach to those in need was accomplished. But this structure also fell victim to the perils of political life. There were often winners and losers, and, in more situations than one might care to enumerate, conflicts so deep and lasting erupted that in some cases congregations were completely split over issues both substantial and trivial.

The church continued to maintain this model of management and mission long after corporate models of work and society shifted. As the twentieth century gave way to the opening of the twenty-first, fewer leisure hours were available for the volunteer service that fueled the growth described above. People were too weary of meetings in the workplace to gear themselves up for meetings in the evening at church, and the inefficiency and routine of most parish meetings structured on the corporate model made it all but impossible to attract vital leaders whose time and ideas were valued. At least this was the experience we faced as leaders in our work in Seattle.

But we had a deeper, more organic problem with maintaining our standard method of parish life. As more and more people experienced the rich intersection of lectionary and life that is The WAY, the pattern of parish ministry meetings for stewardship, fellowship, education, and the like seemed to pale by comparison. People became used to gatherings that *meant* something, where their thoughts and ideas were valued and their spiritual journey was taken seriously. The idea of meeting to meet or meeting because a meeting was scheduled, regardless of whether there was a pertinent agenda, was something a new generation of disciples would no longer tolerate. Add to this the overdose of meetings in the workplace suffered by most members of our community, and the combination began to ring the death knell for the corporate model that had been the mainstay of parish life for years.

Yet, the realities of institutional parish maintenance persisted. Who would shape the vision and mission? Who would pay the bills? How would worship be planned and Sunday school organized? These are, of course, all pressing, pertinent questions around the faithful life of congregational ministry. I've seen a congregation so desperate to preserve institutional maintenance that a first-time visitor—a person who had not been inside a church for more than three decades—was actually recruited to serve on the stewardship and finance committee. It was her first *and* last visit to that particular parish.

A first step in working toward a new model for your congregation might be an honest discussion with parish leadership about the changing shift in the existing paradigm and attitudes mentioned above. Even this discussion should be initiated around a different model. The pastor herself could freely call such an informal gathering, and because of her seminary education, she is uniquely trained to lead this conversation. Gather a small group together that includes "official" and "unofficial" leaders. Light a candle. Say a prayer. Read a Scripture text together, perhaps a reading used in the past Sunday's worship. Then stimulate the discussion by asking the question, "In this text, where do *we* see God leading us in our mission as a congregation?" Limit the discussion time to ninety minutes, keep the conversation on the subject of vision, and reconvene the group around a different text in no more than two week's time.

The Scriptures, infused with the power of the Holy Spirit, will do the work. You can count on it. Certainly there will be details to work out, but this method of parish leadership—doing what the church is uniquely called and qualified to do—will be so inspiring to Christian disciples who are burned out on the corporate model of leadership that the results will immediately become evident.

And what will those results be? They will be as varied as the gifts of the Spirit and as individual as churches large and small. For some, the result will be a model that places more decision-making into the hands of pastors and staff. For others, it may be the genesis of a task-force model of ministry. One thing is certain to occur: a reevaluation of priorities, followed by a blessed release of many institutional patterns and habits that were being unquestioningly maintained rather than the ministry being intentionally focused on mission.

In our situation, a variety of the results noted above emerged. There is no question that the emphasis of decision-making and implementation has shifted to pastors and staff. In parishes with only one pastor on staff, it is conceivable that more decisions will rest with the pastor and/or the parish council.

Many ministries have moved from a committee model to that of a task force. Whereas previously parish members felt trapped by a two- or three-year term of service in which a monthly meeting often produced minimally satisfying results, they now serve on a four- or six-week task force to plan, execute, and evaluate a ministry project or program, and then have the freedom to move on.

Here is a very concrete example of how changing the existing pattern of an organizational meeting in our ministry brought great results. For longer than anyone can remember, the parish executive committee met a week before congregation council to plan the agenda. This meeting was typically held at church at the end of the workday and lasted from sixty to ninety minutes. It involved the four officers of the congregation, the two pastors, and the parish administrator. Getting across town in Seattle at the end of a workday is an arduous task. In the autumn and winter months, it's already been dark for hours. Rain is typical. To be perfectly honest, most of us would rather have been anyplace else than a church meeting at dinnertime when the value seemed negligible. But no one spoke up until we had a mortgage banker serving as our treasurer. "At my office, we'd typically hold a meeting like this via conference call. Would folks here be open to giving that a try so that we could economize on gas, time, and energy?" he asked. No one disagreed. For about two years the meetings were held by conference call, the administrator sending out the proposed agenda, previous month's minutes, and the financial reports in advance. This year, with our newest set of officers installed, we've agreed to forego even the conference call and have everyone respond to the agenda and reports via e-mail if there are questions or additions to discuss. Efficiency isn't everything, of course, but the time we save is remarkable—the seven of us have regained at least two hours of the first Tuesday of every month. In the previous model, although no one said so, we found that *because* many had made such an effort to get to the church (and those of us already working there had *stayed* there), the meetings went on much longer than was necessary. It simply felt like we owed each other more than five minutes after having made such an effort to gather. I imagine there are similar patterns in the lives of many congregations.

Most parish members now find that rather than spending time at corporate-style meetings they are using their volunteer hours to serve on short-range task forces, to volunteer in the food bank, or to become involved in other outreach ministries. And, of course, there is a large group of persons who annually serve Christ as a sponsor or catechist in the annual cycle of The WAY. These men and women are involved in weekly Bible study that is reflective, deep, interactive, and lectionary-based. The work that begins with the texts in Sunday morning worship is continued in Sunday evening study and lives on in the week to come through the shared prayers and insights that grow out of small group reflection.

Several years ago one of our newly baptized Christians and I spent four days consulting with a Lutheran congregation in the Southeast whose leaders felt they might be ready to move into a process such as The WAY. We began our time with them by splitting the council into two groups and leading a Bible study on the text of the Good Samaritan (Luke 10:25–37). Rather than trying to discover what the text "means," we focused on two questions: what is holding you back from reaching out, and what are the oil and bandages *you* would need from God to be prepared to overcome what's holding you back and to begin to reach out? The conversation was rich and robust, but the real revelation came at the end. As with our Sunday evening gatherings with candidates in Seattle, we invited the council members to form a circle, praying for the person on their left, having heard the discussion of each person's dreams and needs. When the prayer concluded, one of the council members quite spontaneously offered, "We have never prayed for one another before."

I don't think that they were unique.

Without a careful look at a congregational pattern of leadership, we can easily be blinded by the routine. The press of parish life is great. There is much to be done, and, faced with the all-too-familiar scenario of a declining mainline Protestant church, many find themselves in a mode of anxiety. This tends to manifest itself in one of two ways. Either the resistance to any sort of change is so great that it seems insurmountable, or every new whim and nuance becomes attractive to the desperate. The latter group—both lay and clergy—is quick to exclaim, "Let's try this!"

While all sorts of unsuccessful innovations and experiments are being tried and discarded, the gifts through which Christ promises to work are often neglected. Many of the innovative and experimental "fixes" are borrowed from the secular world, while the gifts of Scripture and sacrament—gifts that are central to the church's ministry—are overlooked as the best possible resources for parish revitalization.

I know of a congregation in conflict in a neighboring synod that recently spent over $25,000 to have an outside consultant come in to evaluate their ministry and offer recommendations for moving beyond the conflict into a time of new life and faithful ministry. To be sure, there were problems to be solved, and the insights brought by the consultant around conflict management, systems theory, and corporate anxiety were no doubt helpful. But as I looked through the consultant's findings and recommendations, what I found missing from both report and process were recommendations for the use of the means of grace in building up the body of Christ out of the conflict from which they were emerging. No Scripture study. No prayer. No immersion in the gifts of baptism, preaching, holy communion. To be fair, perhaps these were assumptions that were agreed upon before the report was ever offered. But I fear that is not the case. I fear that, borrowing from the models of management and maintenance prevalent in the world, we too often disregard that which is our unique inheritance as the people of God: the love of Jesus Christ made visible in the word proclaimed and the sacraments administered. With these at the center of the life of a congregation—even its organizational life—congregations are freed to do amazing things.

Our parish was fortunate to have a lively relationship with a neighboring Mennonite congregation. Through this relationship, we were blessed to learn the benefits of consensus leadership, a style of decision-making that now permeates almost all of our congregational deliberations. Working conversationally to build a consensus, we have found that one is much more apt to carefully consider the leading of the Holy Spirit in guiding the mission of the congregation. Since no action can be moved forward until all have reached agreement, we have also discovered that sometimes the Spirit leads most clearly through the one dissenting voice. As the conversation continues to explore the options before us, as we pray together and listen to one another, we believe that we more faithfully find a pathway to which the Spirit is guiding us. This style of leadership, rather than Robert's Rules of Order, is typical in most

Mennonite congregations. It is outlined in C. T. Lawrence Butler's work, *On Conflict and Consensus.*[1] Perhaps a conversation with members or leaders in a neighboring Mennonite church would bring valuable insights to any congregational leadership process.

When we engage in the Scriptures, in honest and faithful conversation, in dialogue with one another, and in prayer, the Spirit does not disappoint us. I believe (and it has been my experience) that the restructuring for which we long is well within our reach. It lies in the gifts of Scripture and prayer, lectionary and life. In other words, our longed-for renewal lies in the power of the Word proclaimed, the nurture of weekly Eucharist, and the refreshment of baptism's renewing waters. These are the best tools that we have. It is when the Sunday text meets that Monday task that ministry happens. For us, this was a process of evolution as the congregation became more fully shaped by our immersion in faith formation as a way of being together in ministry. I hope it can be a gift to draw upon from our experiences of the past twenty years.

1. Butler, *On Conflict and Consensus.*

9

The Text at the Center

They came to Jericho. As he and his disciples and a large crowd were leaving Jericho, Bartimaeus son of Timaeus, a blind beggar, was sitting by the roadside. When he heard that it was Jesus of Nazareth, he began to shout out and say, "Jesus, Son of David, have mercy on me!" Many sternly ordered him to be quiet, but he cried out even more loudly, "Son of David, have mercy on me!" Jesus stood still and said, "Call him here." And they called the blind man, saying to him, "Take heart; get up, he is calling you." So throwing off his cloak, he sprang up and came to Jesus. Then Jesus said to him, "What do you want me to do for you?" The blind man said to him, "My teacher, let me see again." Jesus said to him, "Go; your faith has made you well." Immediately he regained his sight and followed him on the way. (Mark 10:46–52)

Gospel for Year B, Lectionary 27
The Nineteenth Sunday after Pentecost in the Revised Common Lectionary

I SUSPECT THAT for most readers this is not a revolutionary thought: the text stands at the center of the Sunday assembly. As a catechumenal congregation, one that emphasizes the important connection between lectionary and life in the formation of faith, the text has moved ever more steadily to the center of all that we say and do in worship. The purpose of this chapter is to illustrate how one might work through a text to place it at the center of one's worship planning process. Ideally, the pastor's preparation of prayer and exegetical work begins before meeting with any musicians or other worship planners. This initial journey through the text will raise some possibilities and unearth some ways of stimulating the imagination of all who are involved in worship planning. This will be helpful if the "all" of the previous sentence is either the pastor alone or a large and diverse worship planning staff. The worship resources of an organ-led, traditional Lutheran congregational setting are presupposed in the approach described here. But its methods will have application across the wide spectrum of worship styles.

Not long ago, I attended a preaching preparation workshop led by the Reverend Dr. Anna Carter Florence. With each text we encountered, she asked us first to go through the text and underline all the verbs. I've found this exercise helpful not only in preaching preparation but also in worship preparation, as it attunes me to the movement and the action of the text. I've found it also helps in forcing me to encounter the text deeply, word for word, in a way that simply reading the text does not. A similar exercise that I've found helpful is to write out the text longhand with a real pen on a real legal pad. Remember those?

With the verb exercise, the passage from Mark now looks like this:

> They <u>came</u> to Jericho. As he and his disciples and a large crowd <u>were leaving</u> Jericho, Bartimaeus son of Timaeus, a blind beggar, <u>was sitting</u> by the roadside. When he <u>heard</u> that it was Jesus of Nazareth, he <u>began to shout out</u> and <u>say</u>, "Jesus, Son of David, <u>have mercy</u> on me!" Many sternly <u>ordered</u> him <u>to be quiet</u>, but he <u>cried out</u> even more loudly, "Son of David, <u>have mercy</u> on me!" Jesus <u>stood</u> still and <u>said</u>, "<u>Call</u> him here." And they <u>called</u> the blind man, <u>saying</u> to him, "<u>Take heart</u>; <u>get up</u>, he <u>is calling</u> you." So <u>throwing off</u> his cloak, he <u>sprang up</u> and <u>came</u> to Jesus. Then Jesus <u>said</u> to him, "What <u>do</u> you <u>want</u> me <u>to do</u> for you?" The blind man <u>said</u> to him, "My teacher, <u>let</u> me <u>see</u> again." Jesus <u>said</u> to him, "<u>Go</u>; your

faith <u>has made</u> you well." Immediately he <u>regained</u> his
sight and <u>followed</u> him on the way.

Each person will notice different things about the text upon
completing this exercise, but here are some of the things that come
to my mind:

1. There is a great variety of movement in the text, sometimes
   even within a sentence or two: *came/were leaving; was sitting/
   got up; throwing off/sprang up; was sitting/followed.*

2. Each of the characters in the story plays a different role: Jesus,
   the disciples, Bartimaeus, the crowd. I begin to ask myself,
   with whom do I relate in this text? With whom will the congregation relate? How and why?

3. There are connections in this text between Bartimaeus' plea
   for healing and the congregation's weekly, ancient song, *Kyrie
   Eleison* ("Lord, have mercy").

4. The title "Son of David" seems unique, and it is used twice.
   What might that mean?

5. I begin to think musically: "Amazing Grace" comes to mind,
   especially the line, "I once was lost but now am found / was
   blind but now I see."

I am also aware of a beautiful gospel motet on this text set by Mel-
chior Vulpius, "Jesus Said to the Blind Man."

With these initial thoughts in mind, I tuck them away in
prayer and planning as a lens through which I'll contemplate the
worship for this particular Sunday. I look forward to conversations
with other staff members and worship planners. Even if one is in a
parish without the benefit of additional staff members, this foundational planning work will yield significant results as the worship
takes shape.

It will not be possible, of course, to incorporate all of these
insights or ideas into a single worship experience. Editing is important. Take heart! The text will return again in three years. Some of
these insights and ideas will seem Spirit-guided for this particular
worship plan, and they are the ones to be explored further and
implemented. In this particular case, let's follow through on two

ideas: the connection to the *Kyrie* and the use of the hymn "Amazing Grace."

Even if, because of worshiping in ordinary time, a congregation were not currently using a setting of the *Kyrie*, this could be a good time to highlight it. Its appearance at worship would in and of itself send a clue to the congregation that something about that text is special today. Is it best to use a setting that is familiar, returning to it like an old friend? Or would it be more striking to use a different setting to highlight the text more significantly? This decision will depend upon what might be most helpful for a particular congregation. Either way, the *Kyrie* could be set into the worship folder with a sidebar-style worship note that helps those gathered in the assembly to make the connection to the Gospel.

Kyrie eleison "Lord, have mercy."	Today's Gospel text uses the words we often sing at this time in the Sunday liturgy: "Lord, have mercy."
Christe eleison "Christ, have mercy."	God's people have cried out to God for mercy across the generations.
Kyrie eleison "Lord, have mercy."	Today in our worship, we join followers of Jesus across the ages who, like Bartimaeus, have come to Jesus in need, crying, "Lord, have mercy." (Mark 10:47–48)

Here are some ways that the Gospel proclamation and the *Kyrie* might be connected. At the time of the Gospel reading, the *Kyrie,* used earlier in the liturgy at the entrance rite, could be repeated. It could now be sung by a soloist, by a choir, or by the entire assembly. Or the words "Lord, have mercy" might be sung prior to and following the reading of the Gospel. Another idea: have the congregation utter the cry of Bartimaeus and sing his very words within the reading of the Gospel itself. Local resources and capabilities will dictate the possibilities.

"Amazing Grace" is not everyone's favorite hymn. This I understand. Yet if ever there were a time when the textual connection was great and the occasion obvious, this would certainly be it. It would be particularly true if you were to share the story of the text with the congregation. John Newton, slave trader, upon encountering a storm at sea, cried out, "Lord, have mercy!"—and forever after knew it was his moment of conversion. From that experience sprang the text of the hymn "Amazing Grace." The connections in worship and preaching are bountiful. Even the retelling of this story in a bulletin sidebar beside the Gospel or Hymn of the Day could be an added gift for a worshiping congregation.

There are abundant resources available from which to draw information about hymn texts and their connection to the biblical texts. Those in the Lutheran tradition will be familiar with the Augsburg Fortress resource *Sundays and Seasons*[1] and its extensive treasury. The same publisher also has very helpful hymnal companions for both the *Lutheran Book of Worship* and *Evangelical Lutheran Worship*.[2] Other volumes of hymn text origins that may be more applicable to other denominations' hymn treasuries are available as well. In addition to these resources that are specifically related to hymns, I have found two others that are quite stimulating to my own thinking and preparation. They also contain inspiring information to share with the congregation. The first is Gail Ramshaw's *Treasures Old and New,* an anthology of the various images that may be found in the lectionary, with bountiful illustrations and connections for the worship planner. The second is a resource that specifically connects scriptural texts to the canon of poetic literature, *Chapters into Verse,* edited by Robert Atwan and Laurance Wieder. Building on Atwan and Wieder's example, I've made my own supplementary collection in a three-ring binder. Whenever I encounter a text—narrative or poetic—that might be useful for future planning I simply clip it and file it in the binder, cross-referenced with the biblical text. Those more technologically savvy might maintain a similar file electronically.

All of these suggestions work together to bring the texts for the day to the center of the congregation's worship life. It is the living Word to which we are joined in baptism that forms the pattern of

1. See http://www.sundaysandseasons.com.

2. The former is authored by Marilyn Kay Stulken, the latter by Paul Westermeyer.

liturgical planning. As God's baptized children, we flow to the font, the pulpit, the table, where the bath, the word, and the meal form us anew as disciples of Christ. And on the wave of our newfound infusion of the gospel, we ride the crest of the baptismal wave into the world to serve for another week.

IO

Worship Preparation and Planning

ANYONE PAYING ATTENTION to worship in the mainline Protestant church over the past thirty years or so knows that, unlike worship in the previous generations of the twentieth century, it has been a time of significant innovation and experimentation. For Protestants on the more liturgical end of the spectrum, the worship plan had always been the worship book. *The Book of Common Prayer*, *The Service Book and Hymnal*, *Lutheran Worship*, or *The Methodist Hymnal* set the norm for a service that was predictable in shape and scope, keyboard led, and familiar in content. For those less liturgical—worshipers in the UCC and its predecessors, American and Southern Baptists, and others—the shape and scope were also predictable, if less structured and usually more locally crafted.

But as the last century gave way to the present one, things changed dramatically—style, scope, and content. These changes can be better analyzed and evaluated elsewhere. The purpose of raising the trend in this particular discussion is this: I hope to point toward the importance of a rich, diverse, and traditional structure to support the work of the baptismally forming community. The character and substance of what happens in worship must be honest and genuine if it is to be taken seriously by those who are inquiring into a life of discipleship in Christ. In a parish where the core curriculum is "lectionary and life," such worship provides the foundational structure in which that curriculum can thrive. It is not a question of style; formational ministry among newcomers to faith and those returning as renewed Christians can flourish in most any setting. It is instead a question of content and authenticity.

I do not mean to imply that worship must be simplistic and instantly accessible. Well-planned, formational worship should be inviting but still offer the assurance that there is something into which one is being invited—something deeper, more profound, and mysterious that is yet to be discovered. A worshiper who is attending liturgy well into their eightieth or ninetieth year should still have the opportunity to experience that there is more about God to encounter. The entire assembly should leave worship longing for our next encounter with the holy, confident that it will be transformative and profound.

What is it that makes liturgy real, authentic, mysterious, and profound? Perhaps an illustration is in order to bring a bit of flesh to the bones of this theoretical conversation. I recently presided at a graveside service of a member in a distant city. I did not know the local customs, the funeral home, or its directors. While driving there I felt a bit nostalgic for the familiar men and women in Seattle who work in the funeral business and with whom I had developed a collegial relationship. Knowing that there could be some unfamiliar territory to navigate, I planned to arrive early—well before any family members or friends had gathered at the gravesite.

My worst fears were confirmed when I walked into the tent that had been erected over the grave and noticed two large wicker hampers off to the left side; one was quite large and the other very small. Upon shaking my hand and welcoming me, the funeral director introduced me to the contents of the wicker hampers—birds that he called "doves." He said, "These will be released at a point of your choosing during the service. You can explain that the first to be released is Roger's spirit dove, and then when I open the second coop, you can explain that all the rest are our spirit doves, following Roger into heaven."

I quickly assured the director that I wouldn't be saying anything about the doves and welcomed him to come forward when my part of the service was concluded to do anything he might like with the doves.

I was not being stubborn or arrogant—or at least I was not trying to be. I felt this was simply a bad symbol, bad theology, and bad practice. It was reaching for something new and innovative to ease the pain and truth of this time of death, but it was neither honest nor theologically sound. This was chancy as an element to be incorporated into one of life's most profound liturgical moments.

In the first place, these were not doves, they were pigeons. Homing pigeons. So, the symbol lacked honesty and integrity from the start. Theologically, the action was in competition with and contradiction to what was happening at the graveside. According to our understanding of the resurrection of the body, no one's spirit was going anywhere. And it was certainly not going there on the wings of a pigeon. Nor were we who had come to mourn following the deceased. Ours was the task of going back into the world in faith and hope to do the work that God still had for us to do.

Sure enough, when the crate of "spirit doves" representing all of us was released, one of the doves—it must have been channeling my discomfort and objections—flew about twelve feet into a Western Red Cedar and spent the rest of the service looking down into our little group.

I recalled on the drive home that it was at this same cemetery years earlier that I had first encountered a similarly unsettling ritual, one in which during the military rites a "bugler" held a horn near his lips as a device buried in the bell produced a prerecorded version of taps. At one of the most sacred moments of a veteran's life, when his body, given up in service to his country, was being placed in the ground, we could not muster a more meaningful way to say our farewells than this faked, lifeless, and cheap gesture. Our rich incarnational theology that teaches God alive among us demands something more.

These might seem like extreme examples, but the point I am making is this: I have observed over the past thirty years of ministry that there is an increasing level of comfort with reaching for the new and the innovative as a way of "keeping interest" and "staying contemporary." No one could be more interested in those goals than I am. But we must always ask, "Keeping interest *in what?*" and "Staying contemporary *to what end?*"

Worship planning and preparation that is worthy of the God to whom it is offered begins with the texts appointed or chosen for the day that tell us the story of our God. Responsible worship planning is biblical. Faith comes from what is heard. So it makes sense that those planning the assembly's worship hear, read, study, pray over, and become thoroughly familiar with the texts, and from those texts allow everything else about the worship's shape and content to be formed. The previous chapter, "The Text at the Center," illustrates one method by which worship planners could approach this task.

The biblical text should have a powerful impact on weekly hymn selection. Here's a concrete example of the power of carefully choosing a hymn text and how its use in worship enriches and builds community. The text in question for the day is the story of Moses and the burning bush, Exodus 3:1–15. Contained in this passage is not only the narrative of Moses' call but also the strong and grounding language of the revelation of God's name—I AM WHO I AM—and the repeated reference to the ancestors of the faith: Abraham, Isaac, and Jacob. A natural selection for a hymn at this liturgy would be "The God of Abr'ham Praise."[1] With its strong and accessible Jewish folk tune, *Yigdal,* and its extensive text filled with allusions to both the Exodus text and the baptismal journey, it is an excellent choice.

But let's face it: for most congregations this is an unfamiliar hymn tune with eight stanzas in a minor key. Simply looking at it on the page can be daunting. But here are ten reasons, expanding on what's already been outlined above, that commend this hymn as a wise choice.

1. It has a direct, reinforcing allusion to the text: "'I Am the One I Am' / by earth and heav'n confessed; I bow and bless the sacred name / forever blest.'"

2. It speaks of the pilgrim journey toward the promised land, a

---

1. *Evangelical Lutheran Worship,* #831.

64

journey that all of God's people—past, present, and future—make: "The goodly land I see / with peace and plenty blessed; the land of sacred liberty and promised rest."

3. It contains rich baptismal language grounded in the exodus story upon which our Christian baptismal liturgy is founded and upon which we may continue building a community theology of formation: "The watery deep I pass / with Jesus in my view."

4. The text further makes a connection to our Jewish ancestors in the faith through its title, "The God of Abr'ham Praise," which echoes the phrase "the God of Abraham, the God of Isaac, and the God of Jacob" we find repeated in Exodus 3.

5. *Yigdal* is a strong and singable Jewish folk tune that can easily be embraced by any singing congregation if thoughtfully introduced.

6. It is a thoroughly doxological hymn in both text and tune.

7. It is a great demonstration of a joyful hymn of praise cast in a minor key.

8. The text inculcates a theology of discipleship: "I all on earth forsake / its wisdom, fame, and pow'r; and you my only portion make / my strength and tower."

9. It is a satisfying, joyful, and rewarding hymn to sing by worshipers of all ages.

10. With its many verses it is a great hymn to sing in alternation between various congregational groups: men, women, children, choir, east side, west side, etc. As such, it gives the opportunity to both sing and listen to a text as an act of praise.

The beauty and strength of this hymn became apparent to me during a lengthy congregational meeting at a previous parish. We had called a "time-out" to count ballots, and I could see that patience was wearing thin. I knew that this hymn was slated to be sung in worship in a few weeks. It was not a hymn the congregation knew. I invited our organist to move to the piano. Everyone stood for a stretch, and I invited them to imagine the joy of a Jewish wedding or family celebration. The piano began the tune and everyone began to clap. Little by little, we all joined in, singing simply, "la, la, la, la, la, la . . ." A few people even shouted "hey!" at the end of each line. I sang them a stanza of the text and they responded with a stanza of "la, la, la, la, la, la . . ." By the time the ballots were counted, everyone was having so much fun that the energy sustained them for the remainder of the meeting. Two weeks later when the hymn was sung in worship, the congregation embraced it as one would embrace an old friend. We really *had* something—a rich and deep treasure that was not simply a "go-to" hymn but a new hymn that helped us all be more present with Moses at the feet of the great I AM. Because we are present with Moses in that encounter on holy ground, the ground of *our* worship became more holy, as well, in ways that were both known and imperceptible. We were connected to something larger than ourselves by this tune and text. We were connected to the living Word, to our forebears in the faith, and to our incarnate God.

Sometimes the smallest gesture in worship can bring theology to life. It is our custom at Phinney Ridge to celebrate the last Sunday after Pentecost, Christ the King Sunday, with a hymn festival. We sing our way through the church year from Advent to Christ the King, choosing a hymn for each season, interspersing the texts assigned by the lectionary in the storytelling of the change of seasons. We narrate throughout the entire liturgy rather than preaching a stand-alone homily at this celebration. The service is arranged in such a way as to tell the story of the life of Jesus Christ, our King. We sing a Christmas hymn to welcome Jesus as a newborn, quickly move to his baptism in the Jordan, and mark his ministry of suffering as the season of Epiphany gives way to Lent. In Holy Week we offer the Words of Institution over holy communion as in the Upper Room. During the singing of three Easter hymns we come forward to receive the Eucharist. We recall the presence of the Spirit empowering us for work in the world in the church's half of the liturgical year. We collect the offerings and pray, concluding the service with a robust rendition of "Crown Him with Many Crowns."

Several years ago, it occurred to us that since we regularly drape our processional cross with fabric in the color of the season for our actual festivals, we could add that drama to this celebration. With each changing season and its hymn, the fabric on the prominently displayed processional cross is changed as well.

What a magnificent addition this simple gesture has been to this already well-loved annual service. The simple act of tenderly and carefully removing one color and adding the new one for the season of celebration to which we have progressed brings a new awareness of our shared journey. One parishioner commented that it is one of her favorite parts of the service: "It is like watching my pastors lovingly vest Jesus as he prepared for each of his ministries for us."

Worship that draws on and speaks to *all* our senses is worship that connects. Even in the smallest congregations, simply taking the time one Sunday to talk about the altar flowers can be a new window into the grace of the living Word, Jesus, among us. By pointing to the flowers' connection to creation, revealing how their beauty and color reinforce the theme of the day, acknowledging the generosity of weekly donors, and underlining that the flowers serve as a reminder of the communion of the saints when given in memory of departed loved ones, we turn something that most would take for granted into a new tool for communicating an aspect of the multi-layered, never-depleted gospel of Jesus.

In this era of big-screen televisions, home theaters, instant access to the Internet, super-sized meals, and life lived large on every front, we are called as proclaimers of the gospel to bring this gospel to life. The point is not merely to outdo the excess of the culture that surrounds us. Our call as God's people is to run *counter to* the culture of excess.

The saving grace of Jesus that we are called to proclaim will speak more eloquently and convincingly when the principles of extravagant grace, beauty, thoughtfulness, and care are at the heart of our planning and our worship. We are a culture whose senses are numbed by the plentitude and variety of resources that assail us every day. With the best imaginations that we can muster for the task of planning, God calls us to use to the best of our ability (as God has) the gifts of water, bread and wine, word, song, prayer, and silence, in order to communicate what words alone cannot convey.

II

Formational Preaching

MOST PREACHING IN North American Christian congregations these days assigns the listener something more to *do*. Formational preaching offers them someone else to *be*.

Grounded as it is in the conviction that baptism gives us a new birth each day, formational preaching is focused on the dialogical tension between the sin that Christ calls us to leave behind and the new life, remade in his image, to which Christ graciously invites us. As Paul Galbreath writes, "Are you interested in changing your life? This is the basic question the church should offer."[1] We find the essence of this transformation in Paul's Second Letter to the Corinthians:

> For the love of Christ urges us on, because we are convinced that one has died for all; therefore all have died. And he died for all, so that those who live might live no longer for themselves, but for him who died and was raised for them.
>
> From now on, therefore, we regard no one from a human point of view; even though we once knew Christ from a human point of view, we know him no longer in that way. So if anyone is in Christ, there is a new creation, everything old has passed away; see, everything has become new. (2 Cor 5:14–17)

1. Galbreath, *Leading Through the Water*, 32.

The proclamation of such a powerful and mysterious gift is difficult to analyze. Yet in preaching to a catechetical community over time, a number of characteristics of proclaiming this transforming baptismal grace have emerged. In the pages that follow, we'll take a look at six of those characteristics as we have experienced them developing over the past twenty years in our community and its preaching. Two sermons will also be provided as examples of the kind of preaching that is offered in the fervent hope of forming faith. The sermons are, again, aimed at inspiring a vision of who we as individuals and a community might *be* in Christ rather than what we might *do* because we are people of faith.

1. Formational preaching is intimately connected to the text or texts for the day.

Whether in a lectionary-based worshipping community or a congregation whose preacher chooses a weekly text or texts, the biblical story must be at the center. In this story the community of faith is told each week, albeit in different ways, how God has been active in the lives of God's people across the span of history. The story of the exodus shows how God's people were formed by coming through the waters out of slavery and into a new life of freedom. The story of the woman at the well recounts the joyous new life offered by Christ to an outsider through the gift of living water. The prodigal son is offered an heir's welcome despite squandering the inheritance and finding himself without welcome in a far country. The Corinthian community is born again by the opportunity to see how important their conduct is in the formation of new Christians: "therefore, if food is a cause of their falling, I will never eat meat, so that I may not cause one of them to fall" (1 Cor 8:13).

Whatever the text may be, the formational preacher's task is to mine the deep treasures of its ancient stories and words and bring them to life in the present community of faith. Preaching is therefore textual *and* contextual, taking seriously both the words and the settings of its hearers in the past and in the present. Somewhere along the line a wise teacher offered an insight that I have never forgotten, although I have, unfortunately, forgotten the one who offered it: "We should read every Scripture as if the address on the outside of the envelope reads, 'Phinney Ridge Lutheran Church, Seattle, Washington.'" These are great words to live by and greater words still by which to preach.

It is difficult to imagine worship in a Christian assembly at which no Scripture is proclaimed or heard. By definition, to gather for worship *means* to hear the Word of God proclaimed. Yet I understand that there are such liturgies in existence, some of them even held in Christian churches. These might be fine gatherings of people, but they are not worshipping communities. They can't be. Without a word, the service lacks the means through which God has promised to act. Such communities focus on what people should do rather than who, re-created by God, they can be. The message tends to be "lead a moral life," "be kind and compassionate," "work hard." The scriptural story that is missing is the harrowed lives of a band of refugee slaves fleeing Pharaoh; the emptiness of the woman at the well, whose five husbands have brought her no fulfillment; and the sorrow of the prodigal son kneeling next to pigs to eat. You can be something else, the gospel promises. Christ will wash you clean and make you new. This is who you are called to *be*. Preaching that offers less than this may be great oratory, but it misses the opportunity to proclaim the Bible's radical gospel story of death and resurrection.

2. Formational preaching embraces ambiguity and mystery. It does not attempt to give all the answers.

Transformation is a mysterious process. It promises no simplistic explanations or irrefutable proofs. It is anchored in the relationship of trust that God longs to have with us and offers us in the incarnate Christ. Being a disciple does not offer a set of guarantees and a blueprint for the future. Paul Galbreath, in his baptismally centered book *Leading through the Water*, offers us the language to embrace the uncertainty of discipleship. He writes, "The image of baptism as a question mark supports the understanding of the Gospel as a lifelong question. Rather than providing easy answers with dogmatic certainty, the Gospel constantly questions our priorities, self-reliance, and actions."[2] Baptismal and formational preaching, therefore, welcomes one into a community of faith that promises support and nurture, no matter what. This is a promise that only Christ can offer, since Christ has overcome all contingencies, even death itself. There is nothing more mysterious than that, and although it cannot be *explained*, we as preachers are called to *proclaim* it with clarity and conviction.

3. Formational preaching is challenging both to preach and to hear.

The masterful wordsmith and homiletician Frederick Buechner summarizes the plight of both preacher and hearer thus: "As much as it is our hope, it is our hopelessness that brings us to church of a Sunday, and any preacher who, whatever else he speaks, does not speak to that hopelessness might as well save his breath."[3] Few of us who preach set out to speak a message about hopelessness—and it is likely that fewer who get out of bed and into clothes to come to worship on Sunday want to listen to one. Yet before there can be the transformative hope of the gospel, there must be the transformative truth of the *need* for the gospel. Therein lies the preacher's weekly challenge. One must be willing to be booed from the pulpit on behalf of Christ in order that Christ can be cheered and ultimately worshiped as the only hero worthy of our everlasting praise. The preaching of this word of hopeless truth, in all its nakedness and despair, is a challenge to proclaim. And those to whom it is preached, if it is to have any impact at all, are called to hear it about *themselves,* not simply about the human community in general. Before the gospel can be good news, it is essential that it be bad news—the worst: without Christ risen from the dead into whom you were baptized and raised by the grace of God, there is no hope at all. None. Formational preaching is challenging to both preach and to hear.

2. Galbreath, *Leading Through the Water*, 9.
3. Buechner, *Telling the Truth*, 55.

4. Formational preaching is highly narrative. It uses narrative to connect the text to the daily vocation of the baptized.

There's nothing I find more satisfying in the handshake line on Sunday morning than the parishioner's heartfelt comment, "You really connected those texts to my life today." That's the goal. Bringing ancient words from a different culture about a radical God who enters the human condition out of sheer love for the creation is a difficult and complicated undertaking. Yet, fueled by the conviction that this biblical word is a *living* Word and confident of the Holy Spirit's presence and power in the endeavor of proclamation, the preacher can come to find great power and satisfaction in the sermon that *connects.* In our seminary homiletics class in the late 1970s the Reverend Dr. Tom Ridenour used to tell us repeatedly, "Preaching that begins in the Bible, stays in the Bible, and ends in the Bible is not biblical preaching." It took me only a moment to memorize his motto, but it has taken me a lifetime to attempt to understand his wisdom.

One of the elements of formational preaching that connects to the daily ministry of the baptized involves a second sort of exegetical work. We preachers are highly trained and highly capable in the work of exegeting a biblical text. But an often overlooked second element is the exegesis of the present surrounding culture into which the sermon will be preached. We must know the culture, and the context—the very lives of the people to whom we preach week in and week out. A formational sermon will be more effective when it understands something of the daily life at Google or Microsoft; the complexity of a soccer game, a music lesson, a homework schedule; the stress of overextended budgets; the heartbreak of alienation from parents or siblings; or the plight of living alone after a partnership of sixty years together ends with the death of one's beloved. All circumstances will be different, of course, but the art of transposing the living Word from the pages of the lectionary text into the lives of beleaguered people longing to live faithfully is at the core of formational preaching.

5. Formational preaching honestly evaluates the human condition of sin and suffering and points to Christ on the cross as our only hope.

In 1978 Herman Stuempfle wrote a short monograph titled *Preaching Law and Gospel.*[4] Despite its being short (and so a quick initial read), its contents bear reflection across a lifetime. Stuempfle asserts that without the conviction of the law, there is no need for the relief of the gospel. But the more complicated part of that easily memorized preaching motto consists of truly disclosing the gospel. It is what Eugene Lowry, in his paradigmatic preaching manual *The Homiletical Plot*, calls "disclosing the key to resolution."[5]

The conviction of formational preaching is that it is only in Christ and in his dying and rising that there is any hope at all for the plagues and perils of the human plight. Jesus takes them to the cross, where they are put to death forever: "We proclaim Christ crucified" (1 Cor 1:23). This is not only a stumbling block to the Jews and foolishness to Gentiles, it is the downfall of many, if not most, postmodern mainline sermons. We simply cannot seem to preach with confidence that Christ died and rose again for us and that—baptized into his death and resurrection—we are all new people. This is what we are called to *be*. But most sermons cannot avoid the temptation to tell the faithful what to *do*. If you hear concluding lines such as "and so, in the week ahead" echoing in your ears from your own preaching, go back and have a second look at how that sermon might end more authentically with the gift of the gospel rather than the task of a new law. If your fingers on the laptop keyboard lead you in the direction of "we need only to," it is worth reexamining your call to action. Honestly assess the proclamation, assuring that who we are called to *be* in Christ is at the center. We as preachers are more apt to give people something to *do* in the Risen Lord's name. "Blessed be the God and Father of our Lord Jesus Christ! By his great mercy he has given us a new birth into a living hope through the resurrection of Jesus Christ from the dead" (1 Pet 1:3). That is the naked promise, in all its straightforwardness

4. Stuempfle, *Preaching Law and Gospel.*
5. Lowry, *The Homiletical Plot.*

and all its complexity, that we are to proclaim each time the assembly gathers.

6. *Formational preaching is targeted more to the community than to the individual.*

Formation in faith by its very definition is a faith lived out in community. The first tier of that community is the weekly, gathered assembly—those hearing the same word proclaimed, being formed by the same words and actions, and eating from the same dishes week in and week out. The concentric circles surrounding this community are those of the larger church extending endlessly across the world and throughout the ages. Our faith is a faith shared and shaped by a community.

But be careful. A faith community is a gathering of individuals, and each person has gifts to bring and gifts to receive from the assembly's worship and service in the world. Luther maintained that two of the most powerful words in the entire liturgy are the words *for you* offered to each communicant at the distribution of the Eucharist.[6] If a person could not receive the bread and cup as a gift offered for each beloved child of God, then how could that person see its value and potential to change her life? I would maintain that this same theological principle applies to the hearing of the word *by each person* within the larger gathering of the congregation. It is not so much an either/or as a both/and. Formational preaching is *more* communal than individual. It is not exclusively communal. Neither is it—if it is to be faithful—ever individualistic.

Here are two examples of formational preaching offered in the recent ministry of our congregation. They are offered in the hope of helping the reader experience some of the characteristics described above, and they will be analyzed at the conclusion of this chapter based on each of the six characteristics of formational preaching.

6. Luther, *Large Catechism*, in *The Book of Concord*, 450.

A SERMON FOR SUNDAY, 26 AUGUST 2012
Lectionary 21, Series B, Revised Common Lectionary

Patrick Meagher
Phinney Ridge Lutheran Church Minister of Outreach

> Joshua 24:1–2a, 14–18
> Ephesians 6:10–20
> John 6:56–69

With today's Scripture readings, the framers of the lectionary assembled a toolkit for cliché-proofing our faith. That is to say, these are not the feel-good passages of God's word.

In the Gospel reading, we hear about a crisis of organizational structure amidst the early Christian church. Jesus wraps up a teaching where he tells his followers to eat his body and drink his blood in order to live forever. The original Greek doesn't allow for listeners then, or readers now, to metaphor away the intensity of this teaching. He means we are to eat his body and drink his blood. Those who heard this were not allowed an escape clause, or really offered any chance to have a different reaction than they did: "This teaching is difficult, who can accept it?" Other versions of Scripture capture more of their great discouragement by translating their reaction as "This is a hard teaching, who can accept it?" A hard teaching. You can imagine their heads shaking as they reconsider their choice to believe and follow this ever-more-unhinged Nazarene woodworker.

Like many of my generation who find comedic delight in awkwardness, I kind of enjoy what happens next. Jesus calls them out: "Oh, does this offend you? Well, hang on because I'm really just getting started." For many of his followers, the ascension preview was a last straw, and they turned back.

I have a friend who writes contemporary liturgical music for churches. A few years ago he was asked to pen a song for Easter morning. The lyrics describe a scene in the afterlife where six million Jews sat at a banquet table with none other than Adolf Hitler. All participants raised their glasses in friendship and forgiveness. Not surprisingly, this image was too offensive for the church to accept. They declined the song. It offends me too; I would probably have made that same decision. But this banquet table image, and how quickly I took offense, have remained with me ever since. My friend's song brought me to the end of my own ability to imagine the Kingdom of God, and invited me to something more expansive. It offered a glimpse of love and restoration my heart just could not accept. It offended me.

God's love is in full bloom when it goes beyond a cliché and when it takes us to the very core of our own disbelief in that love.

All three of today's lessons could carry the label of hard teachings. In Joshua, we see a people being given an ultimatum to put aside all other gods and follow the LORD who brought them this far. Taken at face value, God appears jealous and controlling. Is God really that insecure? The Apostle Paul encourages the Ephesians and us to get ready for a bloody battle. We will need full body armor and are encouraged to use the word of God like a sword on behalf of the gospel. Our faith journey boiled down to a war analogy? For many of us, these are difficult teachings—who can accept them? Most of us, however, are not offended as much by Jesus' teaching about communion. We have two thousand years of familiar tradition to fall back on. We might be a little confused by the mystery, but not really offended. But asking us to fight in the army of a jealous God is a little harder to swallow.

Just as for the disciples, there is a gift for us in these difficult, hard-to-accept teachings.

Sure, we all need to be shaken up a little now and then by a stern warning or an ultimatum or two. But that's not what I mean here; God and his word are way more creative than that. Our gift this morning, and every time we come to God, is to walk away stripped of clichés and disillusions about reality. The reality we're left with may be hard to accept, but it is there and only there we encounter the deep and thick love of God that seeps into every crack of our broken being.

I've come to believe that clichés can be deadly to the Kingdom of God. Love that does not challenge our preconceived, limited ideas about justice and fairness, love that merely confirms the system of shallow relationships that Jesus came to redeem, will only spread the kingdom of earth, and not the Kingdom of God. We desperately need these difficult teachings.

One sublime gift of my work as Minister of Outreach is to hang out with desperate people on a regular basis. I recommend this practice if you need constant reminders of what's real about life, which I certainly do. When a proud man returns, with eyes downcast, asking for a third round of help with a utility bill because of repeated job-market rejection, easy answers are of no use. His children need electricity. An experience many of you share is welcoming a first-time client to our food bank door. Sometimes, she will break down in tears because she never thought she'd be in this situation, and she always has been the one on the other side of the counter helping out. Fielding her frustration, failure, and desperation to feed her family will change your heart. And she draws you closer to your own desperate human frailty and our God who cares for us. These encounters are sacred gifts, but they are not easy to accept.

Fred Rogers, thirty-year host of the PBS show *Mister Rogers' Neighborhood* and ordained Presbyterian minister, once said in an interview with *Christianity Today*, "The things of God are deep and simple, while the things of the world are shallow and complicated." The difficult teachings of Scripture sweep away the shallow and complicated apparatus of faith we sometimes employ, leaving the deep and simple truth of the gospel behind.

That truth is this: The love of God heals everything, *and* that love is for us. It is for you.

And that simple message is the core of today's Gospel passage. Jesus offers his followers nothing less than the path to eternal life. Sure, it's a bit of a weird path with cannibalistic overtones, but an invitation to life nonetheless. Many disciples couldn't accept that path. Those hoping for something more immediate, more useful in the moment, went away disappointed. Peter, the apostolic spokesman, sounds affirmative when he pledges his allegiance to Jesus. These are familiar words, as we sang them today and do so before each Sunday's Gospel reading: "Lord, to whom can we go? You have the words of eternal life." However, I just can't quite discern the tone of Peter's response. Is he affirming his faith out of bold belief, or confessing that they really don't have anywhere else to go? They don't have anything left to fall back on, and at this point they might as well just keep going. The truth may be somewhere in between, especially after this particular difficult teaching, and that strikes me as kind of beautiful. Stripped of easy teachings and shallow answers, it's okay to feel a little unsure following the gospel. This gospel is offensive in how much it loves humanity. Faith sprinkled with hesitancy, fear, resignation—these are all appropriate responses, and God doesn't care if we bring them along too. He just wants *us*.

We may be empty. We may be running on fumes. We may even be happy this morning, yet holding anxiety at bay and feeling very vulnerable about that whole situation. These are the people God wants. We are the people God loves.

Where else in our world can we rest in the message of unconditional love? Where else can we go where we trust that mistakes or character flaws will not wear on a relationship? Where else can we bring every single dark area of our heart? The Kingdom of God— the kingdom of the real. Shallow clichés wither and die in this kingdom. This is why God's love is so offensive to us. Like the man who embodied this love on earth, it is entirely otherworldly.

Jesus calls us as we are and waits with only open arms. Can we accept his teaching?

In the name of the Father, and of the (+) Son, and of the Holy Spirit. Amen.

A SERMON FOR SUNDAY, 30 SEPTEMBER 2012
Lectionary 26, Series B, Revised Common Lectionary

Paul E. Hoffman
Phinney Ridge Lutheran Church Lead Pastor

Numbers 11:4–6, 10–16, 24–29

James 5:13–20
Mark 9:38–50

Are any of you suffering? Pray.
Are any of you cheerful? Sing songs of praise.
Are any of you sick? Call in the church council.
Does your hand cause you to stumble? Cut it off.
Does your foot cause you to stumble? Cut it off.
Does your eye cause you to stumble? Tear it out.

The Bible: It can be so direct. And at the same time, it can be so confusing. The way of life that the book of James lays out seems so straightforward, so reasonable, so, well, *easy*. And then we get to the Gospel and hear these words of Jesus. Equally straightforward. But reasonable? Easy? Not so much.

Let's dig in. For starters, *are* those instructions in James as easy to follow as they first appear? They're certainly straightforward. But let's be honest. When we're suffering, do we pray? When we're cheerful, do we sing a song of praise? When was the last time you were sick and called in *anyone* from the community to pray over you? When I'm suffering, I usually strategize. When I'm cheerful, I often pat myself on the back for a job well done. When I'm sick, I go to the doctor, and then, despite my phenomenal insurance coverage, I groan and complain about the high cost of health care and pharmaceuticals.

And that's precisely the point that brings us to Jesus. "Wake up," the Savior says to us. "May I have your attention? Hell-*o*." You all are so deeply mired in your own habits, your own self-medicating, self-assured self-sufficiency that even when the instructions are as easy as 1-2-3 you are completely lost in your own way of doing things. It's a scandal. It's terrible. Here's how bad it is, Jesus tells us: You are in need of a complete makeover.

Hands. Feet. Eyes. Mind. Heart. The whole thing. You are headed to hell in a handbasket, and the only thing that is going to make any difference at all in your way of living is a resurrection.

"If those feet of yours are leading you down the wrong pathway and carrying you away from me," Jesus says, "then get rid of them. And I will give you new feet. Gospel feet."

"If your eyes are seeing things that are not completely loving and compassionate, if they are filled with specks about how much everyone else is in trouble and missing the beam about how quickly you are going down, then get rid of those eyes. And I will give you new ones. Resurrection eyes. Eyes soothed by the waters of baptism that wake up refreshed and rested each and every day. Eager and longing to serve me—and to see the need to serve the world around you."

Isn't it interesting to see where the scandal that led to these attention-getting words of Jesus all began? It began with a playground fight. The disciples saw people they didn't know who were doing the work of Jesus and they got jealous. They were afraid they just wouldn't be special enough anymore. Their eyes and their hearts were causing them to sin, and Jesus says, "Cut it out. Knock it off." I have given you everything. *Everything.* And the part of that you just can't see is that I came to give that same gift to everyone. *Everyone.* You are really, really, really, really special to me. But you're not that special. You are no more special than anyone else for whom God has poured out an unfathomable store of endless love and compassion. If you can't see that, if you can't walk in that, if your hand can't reach out to embrace that: then cut it out. Cut it out. Knock it off. And in its place let me raise up for you a new hand, and a new eye. A new heart, and a new spirit.

We serve a resurrection Jesus, so no worries when it comes to cutting out our old, sinful millstone of an eye, or hand, or mind, or heart. Jesus will give us a new one. We need a whole new body, a whole new life, a whole new way of seeing and reaching, of walking and thinking and feeling. And our resurrection God will give us just that. This is what we mean when we say, "I believe in the resurrection of the body, and the life of the world to come."

In this season of so many decisions, it's a good thing to keep in mind that Jesus is with us to make all things new. Christ seems absolutely unafraid of stepping into a bold, new future, confident that God will be there to raise him up if and when he falls. The key ingredient in Jesus' way of life is always—always—the boundless love of God poured out as a gift for all God's people everywhere. The "little ones," as Scripture calls them. Those we so often overlook, those without power or privilege, those whose lives are so graciously, consistently lifted up by the strong, courageous, resurrection arms of Jesus. Over and over again.

It was to hell that Jesus took his broken body for you and for me. Broken, weighed down by the sin of the world, he went to that garbage dump outside the walls of Jerusalem, where the worm never dies and the fire is never quenched. It was there, with all the spice and salty seasoning of a confident love, he gave it all away—for us, to us. God has raised us up as all new people: strong-armed, clear-eyed, walking in the way of Jesus, when we are at our best. Sinners, yet saints. Mistaken, yet forgiven. Dead, yet alive to so much possibility through the love of Jesus raised up among us.

In the name of the Father, and of the (+) Son, and of the Holy Spirit. Amen.

∼

These two sermons, with an eye toward their catechumenal congregation, demonstrate a formational preaching style. Below are some specific examples drawn from each sermon that illustrate the six characteristics of formational preaching. As a pastoral staff, we never intentionally set out to write sermons with these six characteristics as guiding principles. But over this first generation of living into being a formational community, we can see in retrospect how these six principles have come to form the basis from which our preaching comes to life. Forming the faith of others has formed us in faith, a faith that from a homiletical point of view has come to be identified by these six characteristics.

1. Formational preaching is intimately connected to the text or texts for the day.

Notice how each sermon immediately incorporates the text or texts read before the assembly for that particular Sunday in the church year. Difficult texts though they are, each of the preachers meets them head on, acknowledges how difficult they are to understand in a present-day context, and goes from there to offer an interpretation for a postmodern congregation. Patrick's sermon goes on at some length exploring the "hard teaching of Jesus" and does not even shy away from its inescapable cannibalistic overtones. This is not the stuff of religious clichés, the sermon asserts. This is a hard teaching. He goes on to include the difficult words of the complementary texts from Joshua and Ephesians. All of it is Scripture, and it is what we are given for today from which to thoughtfully, carefully, and prayerfully mine the gem of the Gospel with which God intends to gift the gathered community.

My sermon begins with the contrasting illustrations taken from James and Mark. James' instruction at first glance appears to be "easy," though that illusion is quickly shattered. The sayings of Jesus from Mark about cutting off offensive body parts are reiterated, and then an interpretation of these challenging and confusing words is offered.

2. Formational preaching embraces ambiguity and mystery. It does not attempt to give all the answers.

The ambiguity of the Hitler banquet table in the first sermon is never resolved. It was preached with honesty and care, but in the end, it simply hangs there. It was a bold and courageous illustration that mirrors the hard teaching of Jesus and so is intended to leave the hearer with the same sort of perplexity that came over the disciples when Jesus spoke equally difficult and ambiguous words.

In the second sermon, the mystery of death and resurrection is proclaimed, not explained. *How* God gives one a new hand or a new eye is left to the imagination. The power is in the mystery of the image, not in the science of its explanation. Nowhere does the sermon attempt to say, "So go get a new hand that looks like this . . ." Rather, there is nothing that is so offensive—in what we see or touch, or in the pathways our wayward feet might travel—that cannot in the end be healed by the baptismal grace of Jesus. This is who we are called to *be*: people who trust in a God who can make them new, since God has promised in Christ that all things are reversible, even the power of sin and death.

3. *Formational preaching is challenging both to preach and to hear.*

As I was writing this sermon, I was mindful of a conversation from many years ago in which someone met me at the door following the reading of this particular passage from Mark and said quite plainly, "I will not be coming back. If you're in the habit of reading those kinds of offensive texts on a Sunday morning, I have better things to do with my time." It had not even been the principle preaching text for the day on that occasion—perhaps that was the problem—but even the hearing of those words of Jesus was cause for a would-be disciple to take offense. This is a dilemma I cannot solve.

I was also mindful of a number of persons who worship in our congregation and are suffering from mental illness. How might these words and what I have to offer concerning them be heard by someone who is ill? The powerful and gut-wrenching opening scene of Wally Lamb's novel *I Know this Much Is True* surged through my mind as I was writing.[7] In that scene, one of the major characters suffering from post-traumatic stress disorder cuts off his hand in a public library because he believes that this is what God wants him to do. What if such a person were in my congregation on the morning I preached this sermon, I wondered. What is my responsibility to *that* listener? Formational preaching is challenging to both preach and to hear.

Yet, it is what we are called to preach. *This* text. *This* day. *This* community of faith. *This* truth about *this* Jesus—not some other, not one softened by our fondest hopes or best imaginations, but the one given to us in the text. Patrick approaches this with care as he acknowledges again and again that this is a *hard* teaching, but it is the teaching offered in the Gospel of John.

7. Lamb, *I Know This Much Is True*, 5–6.

4. Formational preaching is highly narrative. It uses narrative to connect the text to the daily vocation of the baptized.

Both sermons make extensive use of narrative. Patrick shares with the community his work as a minister of outreach—work that he does on their behalf and with their dollars and prayers. The proud man with downcast eyes and the first-time visitor to the food bank come to life in his words because they *are* alive—their experiences are real experiences that the listeners know are authentic and valued in this particular community of faith. They are part of our story. They narrate who we are and what we believe God has called us to be.

Telling my own story of dealing with James' trifecta of suffering, cheer, and sickness catapults the sermon off the pages of the New Testament and into contemporary life. The familiar responses of strategizing rather than praying, patting myself on the back rather than singing praise to God, and going to the doctor (complaining all the way to the office and back) rather than calling for the elders to pray over me are examples meant to share our common experiences as upper-middle-class Christians in Seattle in 2012. This is a description of what we *do*. And it will be challenged as the sermon goes on by who Christ calls us to *be*.

5. Formational preaching honestly evaluates the human condition of sin, pain, and suffering and points to Christ on the cross as our only hope.

"Our gift this morning, and every time we come to God, is to walk away stripped of clichés and disillusions about reality. The reality we're left with may be hard to accept, but it is there and only there we encounter the deep and thick love of God that seeps into every crack of our broken being." This is the assertion of Patrick's sermon that takes us to the cross. In place of our "clichés and disillusions about reality," he proposes the deep and thick love of God, the love we see most richly and fully in the cross of Jesus. It is in death that we are finally stripped of all that separates us from God, but death need not be feared: "For if we have been united with him in a death like his, we shall surely be united with him in a resurrection like his" (Rom 6:5).

Likewise, the second sermon confidently proclaims the cross as the source of the new life Christ offers us. "It was to hell that Jesus took his broken body for you and me. Broken, weighed down by the sin of the world, he went to that garbage dump outside the walls of Jerusalem, where the worm never dies and the fire is never quenched. It was there, with all the spice and salty seasoning of a confident love, he gave it all away—for us, to us. God has raised us up as all new people: strong-armed, clear-eyed people, walking in the way of Jesus when we are at our best. Sinners, yet saints. Mistaken, yet forgiven. Dead, yet alive to so much possibility through the love of Jesus raised up among us." It concludes with the unresolved paradoxes of sinner/saint, mistaken/forgiven, and dead/alive.

6. Formational preaching is targeted more to the community than to the individual.

In formational preaching, the "you" is rarely singular. The preaching is focused on the life of the community, not the moral behavior or personal salvation of any one of its individuals—hence "God raised *us* up as all new people," and "*We* may be empty, *we* may be running on fumes."

In the preaching and the hearing of both sermons, the focus is toward all of us. Each preacher includes himself among those being preached to and thereby heightens the sense of community even more.

With these communal baptismal images, so firmly anchored in the worship life of the catechumenal congregation, God's people are born again and again to return to the world to live out their vocation and *be* the people of God at work in the world. We are God's hands and arms and voices. We are the walking wet.

12

God's Work in the World

FORMATIONAL PREACHING HELPS God's people see who they are. In the language of the previous chapter, it offers us someone else to *be* rather than something else to *do*. As a new creation in Christ, striving to be the body of Christ in the world, those formed in faith engage in a lifelong journey of discovery that begins the moment they emerge from the font and comes to an end in this world with their dying breath. That lifelong journey of discovery is one in which disciples discern how to *be* God's people. How does one go about seeking peace and justice in the world that surrounds them? The promises in the baptismal liturgies in *Evangelical Lutheran Worship* lay that question on the line:

> Do you intend to continue in the covenant God made
> with you in holy baptism
>   . . . to serve all people, following the example of Jesus,
>   . . . and to strive for justice and peace in all the earth?[1]

The clarity of this covenant used over the past thirty years in Lutheran worship has been helpful in broadening the idea of service beyond the church walls. I recall as a mission development pastor in the mid-1980s preparing our congregation's annual Time and Talent response form. For a guy who loves checklists, this duty was a dream come true. Even though there were only about forty

---

1. *Evangelical Lutheran Worship*, 237.

families in our congregation at the time and we were worshiping in
an elementary school cafeteria, I recall that there were about one
hundred different areas of service from which one could choose.
The problem was, they were all jobs *inside* the congregational community, and the great majority of them were geared toward institutional maintenance: usher, choir member, finance committee,
church council, worship setup, volunteer typist. There was another
problem as well: most of the responses were from people already
serving in those capacities. Unfortunately, these massive response
sheets ended up in a file drawer somewhere until they were brought
out as a model for next year's Time and Talent response.

These responses were about what people could do, inside the
church. We had not yet caught the baptismal vision of what one, in
Christ, might be: a disciple living in a baptismal covenant "to serve
all people, following the example of Jesus," and "to strive for justice
and peace in all the earth."

Research tells us that young men and women born between
1980 and 2000 say that looking for a place to serve meaningfully
is one of their top reasons for connecting with a Christian congregation.[2] Our experiences with the recently baptized would confirm
that finding. When one moves from the model of checklists for
Christian tasks to the formation of a lifestyle into which Christ
invites us in baptism, the life that stretches ahead becomes a lively
and Spirit-filled adventure of service to neighbor, community, and
world. The tasks that one might *do* to meet the needs of others grow
out of who one perceives oneself to *be* in Christ, and—grace being
the gift that keeps on giving—the things that one does further form
one as a disciple.

Just a few weeks ago I attended the installation of the bishop
of the Nebraska Synod at which our presiding bishop, the Reverend
Mark Hanson, preached. He reminded us that the gathered assembly at worship is the rehearsal hall for the work of ministry that we
do in the world: "The real liturgy takes place on the streets; what

2. Sevig, "Leading through Service," 25.

we do here is prepare, drawing strength from God, and from one another."[3]

This baptismal view of the connection and interrelationship between worship and service has profound implications for how our liturgies are designed. As worship leaders, we are called to highlight that connection for our congregations in the liturgies we plan. We have the joy of connecting the dots between celebrating the Eucharist, where God feeds us, and the call to feed one another by working to alleviate world hunger. The washing away of our sin in the weekly confession and absolution is a rehearsal for ethical conduct in the marketplace. Hearing the good news proclaimed leads to sharing that news with others, through lives of service that make a difference and transform both the servant and the recipient. We are what we eat, and the conviction of formational faith is that we continue to become for the world what we do and hear, see and touch, taste and smell in the assembly's liturgy. Huub Oosterhuis captures the essence of this theology perfectly in his hymn text "What Is this Place":

> And we accept bread at this table,
> Broken and shared, a living sign.
> Here in this world, dying and living,
> We are each other's bread and wine.[4]

It is not only in the liturgical formation of weekly worship that men, women, and children are equipped to live the gospel in the world. There is a deep and lasting impact to the yearlong small group Bible studies that are a central component of The WAY. Sitting toe to toe with others in a small group and then working and praying with a sponsor, the disciplined encounter with the biblical text forms one as a potter forms clay at the wheel. There is a genuine and weekly *encounter* with the Bible that changes lives. It takes the form of a conversation with the text for the day and a conversation with one's brothers and sisters in Christ. It is *formational*. As disciples sit with one another and consider how God is speaking to them

3. The Reverend Mark Hanson. Installation sermon of Bishop Brian D. Maas, Nebraska Synod, ELCA, September 21, 2012.

4. *Evangelical Lutheran Worship*, #524. Text translated by David Smith.

in this particular Bible text that has fed them at worship, they now begin to imagine how it can fuel them for discipleship in the world. But there is more: accountability. In hearing the texts together in small groups, in struggling with their challenges and rejoicing in their message of compassion and acceptance, brothers and sisters form a community of support. They listen to one another. They pray for one another. They shape the hopes and dreams of one another and share the disappointments and failures that are bound to come to a sinful people. Not only are those new or those seeking renewal in faith called to accountability. The mature in faith are continually challenged and taught by the candidates for baptism. It is a rich fare of *mutual* support. It empowers God's people for ministry in the world—both those who have been in the church for a lifetime and those who are dipping their toes in baptismal waters for the first time. The Syriac Liturgy of Malabar offers its worshipers these words:

> The tongues that sang your holy name now purge of all deception; keep bright the eyes that saw your love and sharpen their perception.[5]

These two brief lines summarize the wonder that we have come to encounter in the miracle of weekly Sundays at The WAY. Having been "watered and fed" at the morning liturgy, the candidates, their sponsors, catechists, and pastors come together on Sunday evening to reflect on liturgy, community, and word. In the rhythm of that encounter our eyes are brightened and our perceptions sharpened. Through God's intimate contact with us and through the loving support of the community, we are empowered to *be* disciples in the world, doing our best to live out the intentions that God has for us as servants who are ordained in baptism, called to a ministry of justice and peace, serving all people, following the example of Jesus.

Ministry in daily life is one of the ancient catechumenate's four core practices. It can be called by a variety of names—baptismal living, the vocation of the baptized, service to the world, social ministry, social justice—but the intent of each name is the same. Through this practice, one takes a newly found life in Christ and puts it into

5. *Evangelical Lutheran Worship,* #497.

action. This final step in the faith apprenticeship is the natural out-growth of the catechumenate's first three practices: worship, prayer, and Scripture study. You have seen in this chapter how each builds upon the other to form new Christians and reform existing ones. The gracious activity of God at work among us calls us to a daily refreshment of our baptismal promises, and to that weekly Sunday renewal in the practice hall of the worshiping community. The waters of each of these streams converge to form a mighty baptismal river flowing from the font to the world.

13

Stewardship

IF I WERE to tell you that a single image transformed our parish's life of stewardship, you would call me either a dreamer or a liar. To some extent you would be correct. Even though I have lived through it, I find it hard to believe that the manner in which we now practice financial stewardship as a people of God could have been transformed by one image. Except for this one thing, the thing that makes it true: the image is completely, totally, 100 percent baptismal. And because of that, it has resonated so deeply within the fabric of who we are as a congregation of the baptized that I hold this image largely responsible for bringing an end to our annual worries about meeting the budget.

It is to Mark Allan Powell that I credit our radical turnaround. If you've read his book *Giving to God*, you know exactly the image that I have in mind. If not, here it is, in brief. But do allow yourself the opportunity to read it in its entirety in Powell's book.[1]

Writing of the Christian missionaries who encountered the Gauls centuries ago, Powell relates the following:

> As the story goes, when a converted warrior was baptized in a river or stream, he would hold one arm high in the air as the missionary dunked him under the water. This seemed a peculiar custom and the missionaries soon

1. Powell, *Giving to God*.

learned the reason for it. When the next battle or skir-
mish broke out, the warlike Gaul could proclaim, "This
arm is not baptized!", grab up his club or sword or ax,
and ride off to destroy his enemy in a most unchristian
manner.[2]

Just so, Powell asserts, we hold our wallets over our heads as we are
baptized. The thinking of postmodern Christians (and those who
lived centuries before us, I would contend!) goes something like
this: "You can have anything of me that you want, but you can't have
my money. In fact, don't even talk to me about it."

Because baptismal images speak so powerfully to those who
populate our congregation, this image made sense. It began to seep
in, and over time it has become a central way of talking and thinking about our stewardship of money in congregational life.

In keeping with our propensity to construct a ritual for every
occasion, we took this image of baptized money and made it a central theme of stewardship preaching and teaching several years ago.
On the Sunday that pledges are offered at our place, it is customary
for people to come in an offertory procession, bringing both that
Sunday's offering and next year's pledge to the altar to be collected
in an offering basin or basket. But on the year that this image came
into our liturgical vocabulary, we filled our large baptismal tub at
the head of the center aisle with water. And beneath that water
we floated all manner of purses and wallets. There were baptized
checks, coins, and cash beneath those waters, too, and atop them a
large bowl awaited the offering that each worshiper brought to add
to the baptismal font. As the offerings were dedicated and prayed
over, waters from an evergreen branch were gently sprinkled over
the worshipers in much the same manner as the asperging waters
of baptism are sprinkled over congregational members at the Easter
Vigil and other baptismal festivals.

The point was unmistakable, and the impact lasting. God
wants all of us, even our money. It is a part of the baptismal covenant in which we live; it is part of who disciples of Jesus are called
to be and a practice by which they are identified. The tangibility of

---

2. Ibid., xi–xii.

this image brought to life a prayer that we had prayed together so often but that until then had lacked a visceral connection:

> We offer with joy and thanksgiving what you have first given us, ourselves, our time, and our possessions, signs of your gracious love. Receive them for the sake of him who offered himself for us, Jesus Christ our Lord. Amen.[3]

This overpowering image—heard, seen, and touched—has helped bring the work of offering God our time, our talents, and particularly *our money* into a whole new perspective that is consistent with the baptismal, formational life of the entire congregation. It is a part of our story, an authentic and real part of what it means to be a baptized child of God who lives in gratitude and thanksgiving.

Recently, the vice president of our congregation council, John, spoke during worship, encouraging each member to prayerfully consider and then offer a pledge for the coming year of ministry. Completely unprompted by any staff member, John related that as his family gathers around their table to talk about their pledge for the coming year, they talk about it as a couple and with their elementary school daughters as a time of celebration. He related the celebration of the annual family financial commitment to the celebration of the Easter Vigil ten years ago at which he and his wife renewed their baptisms. He spoke of the celebration of each of their daughters' baptisms at successive Easter Vigils as they were born again into the family of God. John and Jackie, and for hundreds like them in our parish, the connection between baptismal celebration and giving are inextricably connected.

Of course, the transformation of a congregation's pattern of giving is more complicated and complex than a single image. Yet I would maintain that it is the image's connection to the context and the story of who this congregation understands itself to be that carries so much weight with us. Simply having that image in the minds of lay and pastoral leaders is formative. One need only say in a meeting, a class, or a congregational meeting something along the lines of "looks like we need to be baptizing those wallets" and people nod knowingly.

3. *Lutheran Book of Worship*, 67.

I have led Bible studies for the council in which all the members were invited to lay their wallets on the table, and before the study was concluded, all the wallets were sprinkled with water as a reminder of the baptismal responsibility of stewarding our own and the congregation's money. Subsequent liturgies following that first "baptized wallet and cash" procession have called this theological understanding back to the collective mind of the congregation. We have mentioned it in preaching and reused the illustration in teaching. It is alive among us, and it has changed our perspective and our generosity.

It would be overstating the case to say that Powell's story of the baptized Gaul is the reason we employ automatic withdrawal as a method of first-fruit offerings with such gusto. But it would be fair to say that the image and the story have led us in the direction of understanding the importance of employing such a plan for giving and interpreting it to the congregation as a theologically sound and biblically rich way of making our weekly contributions. It would also be overstating the case to say that the story alone engendered the generosity to allow our congregation in 2011 to give away over $120,000 to benevolent causes outside our parish. But understanding our stewardship toward others—reaching them in love with the gospel of Jesus—has been strengthened by the richness of Powell's illustration. As a formational congregation, we see ourselves connected to the Bible's story through the lens of holy baptism. In the dripping-wet, stubborn Gaul, we more easily see ourselves as that rich young ruler, as the tax collector Zacchaeus, or as the rich man of Jesus' parable who refused generosity to Lazarus.

As pastoral leaders we have long contended that although we participate in a liturgy that is universal, at the same time we hold in tension the truth that all liturgy is local. That is to say that, in concert with the tradition of Christian liturgy across the ages, we take from our ancestors in the faith the basic shape and pattern, adapting it with rites and texts that bring that ancient liturgy to life for a new day. This is one such case. Imagine it—baptized money, offered by baptized children of God, both dripping with the grace of God and offered in service to a world in need.

14

The Shape of Our Prayers

THERE IS A ritual that occurs every year just before the Easter Vigil begins. As the congregation is gathering on the front lawn for the striking of a new fire, the candidates and their sponsors are gathering in the fellowship hall to form the procession behind the unlit paschal candle. From here, we will journey to the front lawn to make the most significant walk of the year together in The WAY. We will encircle the fire pit where a new fire will be struck, the Alpha and Omega proclaimed, and the affirmation chanted three times: "The light of Christ. **Thanks be to God.**"

But first, there will be a prayer. The candidates and their sponsors gather in the fellowship hall, where they form a large circle. We invite them to look into one another's faces, and we say words similar to the following:

> We want you to know that in the faces that you see in this circle, you see the answer to our prayers. We have prayed that God would send you to us, and you have come. You are the living testimony that God is faithful, and we are grateful.
>
> Let us pray.
>
> Gracious God, for these men and women, we give you thanks. We have prayed for them to come among us and you have answered us with their presence. Come with us now as they are made your own in holy baptism and as

we are re-formed in the faith of the Risen Christ. We ask
this through Jesus our Lord. Amen.

We say that prayer in all sincerity, because for months we *have*
been praying in our regular Sunday services that God would lead
"yet more women, men, and children who have not yet heard the
Word of God to come to the savings waters of baptism." It seems
so simple to offer this prayer, yet its incorporation into our regular
liturgy did not come effortlessly. It was in being formed by those
who came to us that we began to see that God was indeed using us
as instruments of the gospel. The prayer of invitation that had been
sighed by the Spirit was now a prayer that we could and should
articulate in words of our own. That transformational experience
of prayer has been but one aspect of the new shape of our prayers
together as God's people.

The rites of The WAY themselves have led us to new dimen-
sions of praying as the people of God. Bringing candidates to the
font regularly for baptism or its affirmation is a communal endeavor. We are all in this together. It is the very nature of baptismal living that we live in community with and for one another. As
the prayers of blessing are said over the candidates each time they
gather around the font in their baptismal journey, the congregation
is invited to extend their hands in blessing for the candidates and
their sponsors. It seems like a small gesture, but it is mighty. And it
is formative. Over a period of years and years of raising our hands
in blessing, we have come to see our hands lifted in prayer as instruments of God's Spirit. They are the means by which God makes
visible the power of God's own welcome and blessing. It is amplified
for the candidates *and for the congregation* when we show that we
are partners in ministry with Christ.

Another of The WAY's rites that has changed our lives of prayer
is the act of anointing. The newly baptized are anointed with oil as a
sign of the Holy Spirit's presence in their lives. The act of anointing
led us to study and understand the use of oil in the church's life, and
to appropriate that gift in our own lives of faith. Baptismal oil led to
healing oil. Healing oil led us to prayer and anointing for healing,
now a regular staple of our congregation's life and practice. While

we offer the opportunity to receive healing prayers and anointing to anyone at any time, on every other Sunday a minister is available in the chapel during the distribution of the Eucharist to offer healing prayers for those who desire them. At the annual celebration of the feast of St. Luke in October, an entire Sunday liturgy is given over to a service of healing prayer, as members of the assembly line up before one of the four healing stations to receive this gift. Such a rite could not have been imagined in the life of our parish in 1990. Yet now women and men, children and youth come eagerly to receive this gift and to pray for healing in their own lives and in the lives of their family members and friends, as well as for healing in our world. It is powerful beyond words to experience children coming to receive healing for "my skinned knee," "my grandma who has cancer," and "politicians who lie and cheat and make wars happen."

The depth and breadth of the children's prayers is not surprising. Intentional efforts to *teach* prayer are incorporated into our Sunday school, our Wednesday evening midweek classes, and our choral rehearsals. Kindergartners through second graders, for example, end each of their weekly Cherub Choir rehearsals with a five-minute ritual in which the room is darkened, candles are lit, and prayers are offered. The wise and caring choral director of these children opens the prayer time with allusions to the texts they have just rehearsed and then allows their prayers to follow. The youth, chancel, and gospel choirs have similar closing rites with shared prayer.

Godly Play Sunday school classes, with their "I wonder" questions and structured beginning and ending rituals, offer a particularly opportune time to teach, model, and pray. Recently, one of our Godly Play instructors sent me a Sunday afternoon e-mail:

> Just to share . . . this morning Aaron asked us to pray for his mom and her cancer. As we prayed it was just natural to start singing "Healer of Our Every Ill" together. Aaron shared in words and gestures how, in the manner of a second grade boy, we can fight fear with strength. It was clear to me the comfort he felt in sharing and praying together. A gift . . . as you well know.

The comfort felt in sharing and praying together in a class of eight or ten second graders grows into the comfort of a congregation sharing and praying together in the sanctuary at public worship. Our regular prayers include a time when names of those for whom we wish to pray are lifted aloud or silently. They also include a time in which any individual's prayers are welcome to be added to the prepared prayers in response to the invitation, "For what else shall the people of God pray this day?" Our weekly worship bulletin contains a lengthy and detailed prayer list for use in liturgy and in home devotion and prayer. The names are listed and the requests stated plainly.

Each of these treasured gifts of prayer can be traced directly to the small group Bible studies that are the mainstay of the Sunday evening WAY gatherings. As the groups build intimacy and trust with one another over time, the prayers move from the lips of the catechists to the lips of the participants. Prayer, a new practice for new Christians, is taught. By the time of intense preparation in the Lenten season, as each small group draws to a close, its participants gather in a circle. After having spent an hour together experiencing a biblical text, the final question to which each group member responds is, what do you need from God for the week ahead? The closing prayer of the group incorporates those requests into a shared prayer as every participant prays for the person on her left. The communal, other-centered life of prayer takes root early in the Christian journey.

All congregations pray, of course. Formational congregations pray with an immediacy and an intensity that gives voice to the very same questions and longings that characterize our journey together as new and re-forming Christians. Our prayers were not composed by someone outside of our community years ago and miles away, edited, published, and sent to us for use on a Sunday morning. They are composed locally, often on Saturday night or Sunday morning so as to incorporate the world's most current needs and joys. They are drawn out of the deepest longings and greatest hopes of *this* community of faith on *this* day in our lives, wrapped around *these* texts and *this* assembly. They are specific to who we are.

Just as the texts for the day stand at the center of proclamation in preaching, so they stand at the center of the formation of our parish prayers. On any given Sunday we might join our voices to the voice of Amos crying for justice, or St. Paul lavishing thanks, or the woman with the twelve-year hemorrhage pleading for healing. In this way, they also bring alive the biblical story and reinforce the presence of Christ with us now. We are united not only with those who worship by our side, but we share the treasure of men and women across the ages and across the world who were washed in the same waters.

15

Faith Shaping Ministry

"For where your treasure is, there will your heart be also."

—Matthew 6:21

EVERYONE LOVES THE joy of a discovery, a fresh treasure to cherish. Our hearts are restless. Most of us are tempted to look anywhere for something new, even when we already have what we need. As people of the gospel of Jesus, the place of the treasure for which we long is not in the new or the different. Our treasure lies buried deep within the waters of baptism where Jesus himself unites us to a death like his and graciously raises us in a resurrection like his. This is not new. But it is a treasure—the most priceless treasure that one could ever imagine.

Remember Brigid from chapter 1? She went skipping to the font for prayer, assured that it was at the font—in baptism—that her faith was grounded. Her heart simply led her there. She already knew as a kindergartener that the treasure of her faith was in the waters. She would have been hard-pressed to articulate the paradoxical theology of death and resurrection. But she knew, because her parents, her church, her weekly worship rituals had all converged to assure her the story of faith both began there and ended there.

Like Brigid before her, Dorothy, almost ninety years of age, came to the waters a few weeks ago as well. It was a long trip for her—all the way down the center aisle from her seat in the back row. She sits back there these days because those seats are closest to the main entrance where the church's van drops her off each week for worship. It is there that she sings the hymns, hears the sermons, and joins her prayers with all of ours. It is there that she waits patiently for the Eucharist to be brought to her by an assisting minister, the journey down the long center aisle being more than she is able to attempt on a regular basis.

So what brought her all the way to the waters a few weeks back? It was pledge Sunday. With every other worshiper, Dorothy lined up to bring her commitment for the coming year of ministry to the font. With her walker gripped firmly in both hands, and her pledge card tight in that same grip, she came forward with the rest of us. Noble, determined, faithful: a living example of discipleship. There with her brothers and sisters in Christ, she placed her pledge in the large offering bowl floating on the waters. She wanted her treasure and her heart to be together. And what better place for them to converge than the place where Jesus Christ, life's true and only treasure, had first converged with her—at the font of her baptism?

The treasures for which we long are not far from us. They are not new or trendy. They lie deep within the gifts we've always had in the church. They are in our Scripture and our tradition. It is in these that the story of Jesus—told and retold—assures us that our lives, too, are formed as Christ's was. Our lives are formed by dying and rising.

The Bible story of Jesus is a story that never wears thin, never gets old, never can be fully mined of its riches. That is the very nature of what Luther called the *viva vox*, the living Word. The treasure for which we long lies in lectionary and life—in the Bible text cracked open week after week in the assembly of the faithful, and in the tradition of the life experiences of God's people, stretching from Eve and Adam to the newest babe in arms worshiping in our pews.

This sacred treasure is entrusted *to us*, frail earthen vessels that we are. Pastors, people, Brigids, Dorothys: all of us together are united with Christ through this story in his beloved body, the Church.

Through my experiences at Phinney Ridge in Seattle, I have come to develop a core conviction. The conviction is this: when we reach deep *within* the treasures of the ancient liturgies and texts of the Church, we find the transformation that Christ promises us in our baptism. Buried deep within those storied waters, treasures to build our faith abound. Each weekly gathering gives us the opportunity to experience these treasures more deeply than we did the Sunday before. Week in and week out we see God active among us in ways we could never anticipate. There are no substitutes for the resources God has given us: Word and water, wine and wheat, font, table, pulpit, prayer and sermon, song and silence. The baptismal mystery resides in these. It comes to life as we gather for worship and praise. In these extraordinary, ordinary gifts we are shown again and again the crucified Christ being raised up to new life among us. For us. United with Christ in a death like his, we are raised up with him to a resurrection like his. There are no more precious gifts than these for forming faith and shaping ministry.

Appendix 1

Sixth Grade Confirmation Instruction Story Log

THE FOLLOWING STORIES ARE those generally used, following the pattern of the church year. Accommodations are made for the gender makeup of the class and their theological and developmental engagement.

"The Welcome Table" by Alice Walker

"Those Three Wishes" by Judith Gorog

"Right Off the Bat" by Jim Trelese

"The Sneetches" by Dr. Seuss

"Death of a Fish" by Adam Gopnik

"Regret" by Kate Chopin

"A Stag Looking into Water" by Aesop

The Lost Sheep, the Lost Coin, the Prodigal Son (Luke 15)

"A Quiet Chamber Kept for Thee" by Walter Wangerin

"The First Christmas Tree" by Eugene Field

"The Gift of the Magi" by O. Henry

The Christmas Story (Luke 2)

"The Lottery" by Shirley Jackson

"Remember that You Are Dust" by Paul Hoffman

APPENDIX 1

"Little Things Make Big Differences" by John and Monique Nunes

"Material World" by Peter Menzel

"Ragman" by Walter Wangerin

The Parable of the Two Sons (Matt 21:28–31)

The Passion Story of Jesus (any of the Gospels)

"Lily" by Walter Wangerin

"The Swede" by Alden R. Carter

"Sister Anne's Hands" by Marybeth Lorbiecki

"The Problem with Polly" by Scott William Carter

"Tear Soup" by Pat Schwiebert and Church DeKlyen

"The Welcome Table" by Alice Walker (repeated)

Appendix 2

Preparing to Affirm

THE FOLLOWING ARE THE open-ended case stories that are used each week in eighth grade confirmation ministry. These are referred to in chapter 5. Each story corresponds with one of the affirmations of faith that the students will publicly make on the day of their confirmation in worship. These promises are drawn from the ELCA's primary worship resource, *Evangelical Lutheran Worship*.

> *You have made public profession of your faith. Do you intend to continue in the covenant God made with you in holy baptism?*
>> *to live among God's faithful people,*
>> *to hear the word of God and share in the Lord's supper,*
>> *to proclaim the good news of God in Christ through word and deed,*
>> *to serve all people, following the example of Jesus,*
>> *to strive for justice and peace in all the earth?*
>
> I do, and I ask God to help and guide me.[1]

---

1. *Evangelical Lutheran Worship*, 237

Week 1
The Promises of Affirmation of Baptism

> *You have made public profession of your faith. Do you intend to continue in the covenant God made with you in holy baptism?*
>
> *to live among God's faithful people. . .*

YOU ARE AT THE end of your first year in college—the University of Washington. What an eye-opening year this has been for you. You have met many new people with different ideas, different backgrounds, and different faiths, including lots of people who say they have no faith at all.

It's time to make some housing decisions about next year. Will you live in the dorm again? An apartment? Move back home to save money?

An acquaintance from your floor in the current dorm approaches you one night at dinner. She asks you if you've made a housing decision for next year yet, and then makes this offer: Five others, looking for a sixth (that would be you!), are planning to live together in a small apartment that has three bedrooms. The first are an unmarried heterosexual couple who will share the first bedroom. The person talking to you doesn't mention anything about their faith. The second two are a Muslim and a Buddhist—two men—who will share a room. There is a fifth person of your gender who still needs a roommate.

Your response about all this is . . .

Week 2
The Promises of Affirmation of Baptism

You have made public profession of your faith. Do you intend to continue in the covenant God made with you in holy baptism?
  to hear the Word of God and share in the Lord's supper . . .

I T'S YOUR SENIOR YEAR of high school. You can't believe your schedule: soccer, crew, homework, social life. And on top of everything else, every adult in your life has been bugging you about getting your college applications sent in before the deadline. The stress and the pressure are unbelievable.

At the same time, you have become really bored with church. It's the same thing every week. Same songs. Same people. Same sermons. What a drag. Or at least that's how it seems to you.

With everything else that has been going on, you've found that it's just much more rewarding (or at least easier!) on Sunday mornings to sleep in a little bit, and then head out to the local coffee shop and chill with friends, work on your essay for your college application, catch up on some homework, or just sip on a mocha and daydream.

One Tuesday after school you bump into a woman from your church who used to teach in your confirmation class. "Hey, I haven't seen you around church for a while," she says. "What have you been up to?"

You say . . .

APPENDIX 2

Week 3
The Promises of Affirmation of Baptism

You have made public profession of your faith. Do you intend to continue in the covenant God made with you in holy baptism?

to proclaim the Good News of Jesus Christ through word and deed . . .

IT'S THE USUAL HUBBUB at the lockers in the morning. The difference this morning is that Mary, whose locker is next to yours, isn't around. She's always on time, or else calls or texts you to let you know she's going to be late.

The first bell rings, and you wait in the hall thinking maybe once some folks clear out you'll be able to spot her. And you're right. As the crowd thins out, you see her coming down the hallway—and she looks terrible. She hasn't washed her hair this morning, she looks like she's gotten no sleep at all, and you—being as good a friend as you are—can tell she's been crying.

"What's the matter with you, Mary?" you ask. "You look like your dad just died."

"He did," she responds. "He was working on his car in the garage last night and had a terrible heart attack. He was dead before the paramedics ever even got there. I don't know what we're going to do without my dad."

She falls into your arms, crying.

You . . .

Week 4
The Promises of Affirmation of Baptism

You have made public profession of your faith. Do you intend to continue in the covenant God made with you in holy baptism?
  to serve all people, following the example of Jesus . . .

AFTER WORKING FOR FOUR years as a teacher in Seattle's pub-lic schools, you have just completed your master's degree in education. And it's a good thing (even though it took two years of night classes)—you now have a wife and two little children to provide for. The bump up on the salary schedule will be great.

One day, as your family is coming out of church, the pastor takes you aside. "I wonder if you could meet me for coffee some-time this coming week?" she asks.

Your curiosity is really piqued.

At your meeting, the pastor says, "I know you're a busy per-son, so I'll get right to the point. Our church needs some folks who are willing to move to Slovakia for a couple of years as volunteers to teach English. I couldn't help thinking of you. The job really doesn't pay much; you're basically a volunteer. But while you're there, there will be free housing and health care, and enough for your family to get by. It could be quite an adventure."

You say . . .

Week 5
The Promises of Affirmation of Baptism

You have made public profession of your faith. Do you intend to continue in the covenant God made with you in holy baptism?
    to strive for justice and peace in all the earth . . .

THERE'S THIS KID AT school who just drives you crazy. Actually, he pretty much drives everyone crazy. Here's his deal: he's late for class, disruptive or rude to the teacher, or somehow or another a problem. And he's been inserting himself into your conversations with others—joining you at the lunch table, then taking over the conversation—and following you home from school and wanting to come in. You get the picture.

It's no secret that he is disliked by many, especially in your circle of friends.

One day after school, you are walking home and see something unusual at the end of a side street, kind of out of sight. The sounds are not encouraging, and even though you're a little bit scared of what you might find, you move slowly toward the action. When you get close enough, you see three older, bigger kids beating this guy up and yelling stuff like, "This'll teach you to interrupt our conversation, you #%$!" Or, "Take that, you rude #%$!"

Your first thought—honestly—is, "Finally! He's getting what's coming to him."

But then you . . .

APPENDIX 3

Walking with Christ

A Spiritual Formation Model for Pre-Marital Counseling

THIS MODEL FOR PRE-MARITAL counseling is intended to empower pastors to assist couples in their marriage preparation by employing the Church's unique gifts. It is designed to help them ground their marriage in the Scriptures and prayer.

The resources may seem Spartan, for the process is spare. Plan for six conversations lasting approximately fifty minutes. Begin and end each one with a ritual such as the one suggested, and plan on gifting the couple with a copy of the Bible on their first visit. You will also need a candle and an extra measure of patience for silent moments as the Word of God visits the hearts and minds of those preparing for marriage with new and valuable insights.

PART ONE: *OPENING RITUAL*

Light a candle and say:

PASTOR: In the name of the Father, and of the (+) Son, and of the Holy Spirit.

COUPLE: Amen.

PASTOR: The Lord be with you.

COUPLE: And also with you.

PASTOR: Let us pray. Gracious and loving God, as you have promised, we know that your Spirit is with us. Help us in our time together to be aware of that Spirit, and through its power may your Word be alive in us.

ALL: Amen.

PART TWO: *SPIRITUAL DIRECTION*

The pastor reads the Scriptures aloud as the couple follows along in their Bible. As in any spiritual direction, the couple is invited to reflect on and explore the leading of the Holy Spirit in opening these words of Scripture to and for them. The pastor asks a beginning question: "What are the insights to which God is leading you today as you read these words together?"

The couple may or may not be easily guided toward the topics listed under each session's heading. Sooner or later, however, each of them is discussed as is necessary, and as the Holy Spirit provides the guidance.

PART THREE: *CLOSING PRAYER*

The couple and pastor hold hands and pray aloud together. For many couples, the first session will be their first experience in shared prayer. As the sessions continue, the prayers come more easily and become more fluent. The couple's words will acquire a new meaning and depth. No verbal prayer should ever be coerced from any member of the threesome. Be sure to remind the couple that they have the option to pray silently. Following the prayers, complete the session by saying:

PASTOR: Let us bless the Lord.

COUPLE: Thanks be to God.

Walking with Christ

THE SPIRITUAL DIRECTION SESSIONS
A Suggested Outline with Scripture Passages

Session One   John 15:1–17
Love one another as I have loved you

> Possible topics: The Challenges of Growing Together
> Life-Giving Decisions
> Children, Families, Friends

Session Two   Genesis 1:26–31
God creates humanity and gives them dominion

> Possible topics: Stewardship of Self, Others, Resources
> Vocation and Leisure
> Balance

Session Three   Ephesians 5:15–33
Love one another as Christ loves the Church

> Possible topics: Role Relationship
> Sexuality, Self-Giving

Session Four   Romans 5:1–11
We find peace in the reconciliation Christ gives us

> Possible topics: Reconciliation, Forgiveness, and New Life
> Conflict Resolution
> Communication

Session Five   Psalm 90:1–17
The psalmist prays for God's favor throughout a lifetime

> Possible topics: Aging and Caregiving
> Giving Voice to Changing Expectations

Session Six   1 Peter 2:4–10
You are God's people

> Possible topics: Faith Journeys
> Becoming a "Church of Two"
> Being a Part of the Community of Christ

A neighboring priest suggested an additional experience of enrichment in prayer as the couple is married. Invite those who attend the wedding rehearsal to write a prayer request for the couple on an index card. Collect those wishes and include them in the prayers for the service at the couple's wedding the next day. In this way, it is truly the prayers of the people that are being lifted at the time of their marriage. Those who have written the prayers for the wedding liturgy are those who have the closest and longest-lasting relationship to this new husband and wife.

Bibliography

Atwan, Robert, and Laurance Wieder. *Chapters into Verse: Poetry in English Inspired by the Bible*. 2 vols. Oxford: Oxford University Press, 1993.

Bass, Diana Butler. *Christianity after Religion: The End of Church and the Birth of a New Spiritual Awakening*. New York: HarperOne, 2012.

———. *Christianity for the Rest of Us: How the Neighborhood Church Is Transforming the Faith*. San Francisco: HarperSanFrancisco, 2006.

Bauermeister, Paul. "Anatomy of Intimacy: Marriage for Christians." *Currents in Theology and Mission* 10 (1983) 283–90.

The Book of Concord: The Confessions of the Evangelical Lutheran Church. Translated and edited by Theodore G. Tappert, in collaboration with Jaroslav Pelikan, Robert H. Fischer, and Arthur C. Piepkorn. Philadelphia: Fortress, 1959

Buechner, Frederick. *Telling the Truth: The Gospel as Tragedy, Comedy, and Fairy Tale*. New York: Harper & Row, 1977.

Butler, C. T. Lawrence. *On Conflict and Consensus*. Takoma Park, MD: Food Not Bombs, 1987.

Evangelical Lutheran Worship. Minneapolis: Augsburg Fortress, 2006.

Galbreath, Paul. *Leading Through the Water*. Herndon, VA: Alban Institute, 2011.

Killen, Patricia O'Connell, and Mark Silk, editors. *Religion and Public Life in the Pacific Northwest: The None Zone*. Walnut Creek, CA: AltaMira, 2004.

Kreider, Alan. *The Change of Conversion and the Origin of Christendom*. Harrisburg, PA: Trinity, 1999.

Lamb, Wally. *I Know This Much Is True*. New York: HarperCollins, 1998.

Lowry, Eugene L. *The Homiletical Plot: The Sermon as Narrative Art Form*. Atlanta: John Knox, 1980.

Lutheran Book of Worship. Minneapolis: Fortress, 1978.

Powell, Mark Allan. *Giving to God: The Bible's Good News about Living a Generous Life*. Grand Rapids: Eerdmans, 2006.

Ramshaw, Gail. *Treasures Old and New: Images in the Lectionary*. Minneapolis: Fortress, 2002.

Bibliography

Satterlee, Craig A., and Lester Ruth. *Creative Preaching on the Sacraments.* Nashville: Discipleship Resources, 2001.

Sevig, Julie B. "Leading through Service: Young Adults Choose Volunteer Opportunities over Worship." *The Lutheran,* August 2012, 25.

Stuempfle, Herman G., Jr. *Preaching Law and Gospel.* Philadelphia: Fortress, 1978.

Stulken, Mary Kay. *Hymnal Companion to the Lutheran Book of Worship.* Philadelphia: Fortress, 1981.

Turner, Paul. *The Hallelujah Highway: A History of the Catechumenate.* Chicago: Liturgy Training Publications, 2000.

Westermeyer, Paul. *Hymnal Companion to Evangelical Lutheran Worship.* Minneapolis: Fortress, 2010.

With One Voice: A Lutheran Resource for Worship. Minneapolis: Augsburg Fortress, 1995.